SOCIALIST HIST(

SOCIALIST HISTORY
OCCASIONAL PUBLICATION
No 31

CLARA ZETKIN

NATIONAL AND INTERNATIONAL CONTEXTS

MARILYN J BOXER

JOHN S PARTINGTON

(editors)

2013

Published by the Socialist History Society, 2013

© Marilyn J Boxer, Florence Hervé, Natalia Novikova,
John S Partington, Susan Zimmermann

ISBN 978-0-9555138-7-9

Typeset by SHS, 2012

www.socialisthistorysociety.co.uk

Clara Zetkin: National and International Contexts

Contents

List of Abbreviations

ADF	Archiv der deutschen Frauenbewegung
APP	Archives de la préfecture de police
BSP	British Socialist Party
Comintern	Communist (Third) International
CPGB	Communist Party of Great Britain
DGB	German Federation of Trade Unions
DKP	German Communist Party
FRG	Federal Republic of Germany (West Germany)
GDR	German Democratic Republic (East Germany)
IFRWH	International Federation for Research in Women's History
ILP	Independent Labour Party
ISB	International Socialist Bureau
IWD	International Women's Day
IWSA	International Woman Suffrage Alliance
KPD	Communist Party of Germany
MOPR	International Red Aid
Nazi Party	National Socialist German Workers' Party
PCF	French Communist Party
PDS	Party of Democratic Socialism
POF	French Workers' Party
POSR	Parti ouvrier socialiste révolutionnaire
PSI	Italian Socialist Party
PPS	Polish Socialist Party
RGASPI	Russian State Archive of Social and Political History
RSDLP	Russian Social Democratic Labour Party
SAPMO-BArch	Stiftung Archiv der Parteien und Massenorganisationen im Bundesarchiv, Berlin
SED	Socialist Unity Party of Germany
SDF/SDP	Social Democratic Federation/Social Democratic Party
SDKPiL	Social Democracy of the Kingdom of Poland and of Lithuania
SFIO	French Section of the Workers' International
SPD	Social Democratic Party of Germany
SWI	Socialist Women's International
TUC	Trades Union Congress
USPD	Independent Social Democratic Party of Germany
WLL	Women's Labour League
Zhenotdel	Women's Section of the Central Committee of the Bolshevik Party

Clara Zetkin in Retrospect: An Introduction

Marilyn J Boxer

It seems useful to open this special collection of essays on Clara Zetkin (1857-1933) by asking why, although once probably the best known woman socialist in the world, she remains so little known today, especially outside the former Soviet Union.[1] One might answer that unlike Louise Michel, she is associated with no singular event as famous as the Paris Commune of 1871, and unlike Rosa Luxemburg in 1919, she suffered no assassination or martyrdom at the hands of proto-nazis. Unlike Alexandra Kollontai as well, she rose to no cabinet position or ambassadorial eminence. Beginning in her own lifetime and continuing into the twenty-first century, she has been the subject of numerous memoirs and biographies, none of which have been translated into English.[2] While she enjoyed a degree of fame in Europe and the United States during the heyday of second-wave feminism, and was the subject of a Columbia University dissertation in 1975, and was discussed in several others, none of that work resulted in an English-language biography.

For inspiring this current publication, we must thank the organisers of the International Federation for Research in Women's History (IFRWH) that met in Amsterdam in August 2010, alongside the quinquennial conference of the International Congress of Historical Sciences. The IFRWH, which in its call for papers suggested Zetkin as a possible topic of interest, also staged an exhibition of Zetkin memorabilia from the collections of Aletta, the home of the International Archives for the Women's Movement, where the women's history meetings took place. Impelled by the date, which was the centennial of the second international conference of socialist women (or, Socialist Women's International, SWI) that met in Copenhagen in August 1910 just prior to the meeting of the Second International, an international panel of historians addressed the question of Zetkin's legacy. The essays included here owe their origins to that event.

For it was there in Copenhagen a century earlier that Zetkin proposed the resolution that led to the establishment of International Women's Day (IWD), which is now celebrated in more than one hundred countries around the world, although its socialist heritage is often forgotten.[3] Three years earlier in Stuttgart, at the first of the SWI conferences convened by Zetkin, the international secretary had sought to finesse internal conflict over the question of women's suffrage, which had become politically vexatious for socialists because it forced socialist parties in several countries where working-class men still lacked the vote to choose between support for class or gender equality. Susan Zimmermann has demonstrated how Zetkin navigated the politics of the Second International as it dealt with this pressing question of universal versus 'unisexual' (male-only) suffrage, while also responding implicitly to international women's suffrage organisations.[4] As a result of her efforts, women's suffrage was included in the socialist programme.

But Zetkin's political career drew her in many directions, and she participated on an international stage in shaping many of the most pressing issues in the left-leaning movements of her time. The first four essays in this collection focus on Zetkin's life and work in four different national contexts – France, Great Britain, Russia and Germany – that underlay her internationalism. They follow Zetkin from her entrance into the politics of the Second International at its very foundation in 1889, through her unsuccessful efforts during the First World War to move her colleagues in belligerent nations to fulfil their anti-militarist pledges, and her consequent movement into the Third International founded by the Bolsheviks after the war, and her later life and death in the Soviet Union. The final essay examines her contributions as an internationalist, showing how Zetkin and the SWI dealt with questions of national representation in socialist organisations and issues of war, peace and imperialism in the context of both domestic and global inequality.

Zetkin began her international career very early. As a young woman she had travelled with a Russian classmate from her native Saxony to Russia, partnered with a Russian revolutionary exile she met in Leipzig, and escaped Bismarck's anti-socialist laws of 1878 by brief sojourns in Austria and Switzerland. But, as Marilyn J Boxer points out in her essay, it was in Paris, where Zetkin lived from 1882 until the expiration of those laws in 1890 allowed her to return to Germany, that she began her career as a public speaker, journalist and international socialist leader. Thanks to the acquaintances she made among socialists from many European countries then living in the French capital, Zetkin added to her already substantial linguistic abilities and knowledge of revolutionary movements. The privations she suffered during the years of exile – her experience of proletarian life – also helped her establish the credibility and moral authority that underlay her successful bid for leadership.[5] Sometimes compared negatively to her more famous close friend, Rosa Luxemburg, Zetkin was described by Luxemburg's biographer J.P. Nettl as an 'intellectually lesser figure', interested primarily in women's issues.[6] In fact, she had wide-ranging interests. While she often addresses herself directly to women, her concerns are with the political and economic structures that create the context for women's lives. Described by Nettl also as 'hypersensitive, often obstinate', Zetkin seems to have tried to integrate her personal life, her political philosophy and her work.[7] Early on she faced the trials of a working single mother of limited means and she spoke and wrote persuasively of women's struggles and needs.

By the second decade of the century, as the threat of a Europe-wide conflict impended, Zetkin turned to what she repeatedly called a 'war against war' as her primary focus. Having addressed British socialists with a strong anti-war, anti-imperialist message as early as 1900 (during the Second Boer War), she now redoubled her efforts. Zetkin saw in international conflict only profits for capitalists and pain for the proletariat. Whether paying inflated wartime prices for the necessities of life, or facing injury and death on the battlefield, they could only suffer. Women especially had a mission to protect and nurture the life that they had created. Drawing on relationships Zetkin established during four previous visits to the island nation, John S Partington shows that between 1912 and 1915 Zetkin wrote anti-war appeals that were published in a number of English-language journals; and she succeeded in attracting British delegates to the international socialist conferences in Basle and Berne, held in 1912 and 1915, respectively, where she presented her famous appeal to socialist women of all nations, as 'Comrades and Sisters', to organise to stop the conflagration.[8]

With the coming of war, Zetkin's principled fight against militarism landed her in jail. Unable, with her anti-war colleagues in the Social Democratic Party of Germany (SPD), to head off 'social patriotism' in her own land, she continued during the war to mobilise forces against it. Using the international outreach provided by her dual position as secretary of the SWI and as editor for a quarter century of the socialist journal for women, *Die Gleichheit* (Equality), Zetkin was the first to convene an international meeting of delegates from belligerent countries, at Berne in late March 1915. Drawing on British journals that followed Zetkin's anti-war activities closely, Partington shows how, having defied her party and 'social patriots' to work across military lines, she became a major presence in the peace movement among British socialists. In presenting selections from Zetkin's letters and speeches, Partington illustrates the vivid imagery – for example, describing war profiteers as those 'who fish guineas out of the blood-streams on the battlefields' – and the powerful elocution that made Zetkin such a persuasive orator.

Most accounts of Zetkin's work available in English focus on her pre-war, socialist period, especially her leadership of the SWI, and the wartime anti-militarism that brought her break with the majority SPD. With the collapse of the Second International and the postwar creation of the Third International, Zetkin's career moved into its final phase, her years as a founding member of the Communist Party of Germany (KPD), and her election and continuous service as its delegate in the Reichstag. Less has been available about her self-imposed exile to the Soviet Union. In the third essay in this collection, Natalia Novikova describes Zetkin's reception by and influence on Bolshevik leaders during the early years of soviet rule, noting especially her influence on Alexandra Kollontai. Drawing on archival materials not available until the 1990s, Novikova expands our knowledge of Zetkin's role as mentor, colleague and soviet propagandist. She also weighs in on the controversy over Zetkin's position vis-à-vis the Bolshevik regime during the final years of her life. Whatever her feelings about Lenin, Stalin, Trotsky and party politics, Zetkin chose to spend her last years in the Soviet Union, where she could at least on the surface witness the realisation of her revolutionary dream.

Zetkin continued to serve the KPD, famously as the presiding officer at the opening of the last German legislature before its destruction by Hitler, where she used her platform to inveigh against fascism. But Zetkin opted for life in Moscow and its environs to living amid the political turmoil of interwar Germany, where the abortive Spartacus revolution and its consequences, including the assassination of Luxemburg, would have made life difficult for her. Physically ailing, she enjoyed in revolutionary Russia the special treatment of a high-ranking official. Despite age and ill health, she travelled extensively as a popular, even inspirational, spokesperson for the Soviet government. The welcome she received, for instance, on a 1924 trip to Baku was recently recalled in a publication of the Azerbaijan Gender Information Center.[9] The accolades she earned can be seen today in the vast array of monuments and public spaces that continue to bear her image and name. While recent biographers suggest that Zetkin did realise the gap between her hopes for the socialist revolution and the soviet reality, Zetkin nevertheless remained a devoted 'soldier of the revolution', as she once described herself.[10] She received the highest honours the Soviet Union could bestow. IWD, her contribution in 1910 to resolving the conflict between socialist and suffragist goals, remains one of three national holidays in Russia.

Zetkin began her career in exile and she ended it in exile. As an internationalist, journalist and unwavering advocate for socialist and anti-militarist principles, she inspired followers in many lands.[11] She also stimulated opposition, including many among the non-socialist feminists whom she disdained.[12] But it was in her native Germany that Zetkin's heritage developed in the most dramatically dichotomous ways. As Florence Hervé shows in the fourth of these essays, during the era of the two Germanies Zetkin was alternately loved and hated in the Democratic Republic and the Federal Republic, respectively. Even after reunification, in 1994 the German Chancellor himself intervened to make sure that a street in Berlin near the Reichstag would not retain her name.[13] In the East, all manner of institutions and public venues bear her name. Providing much information of interest, new especially to non-German readers, Hervé here summarises her extensive earlier publications to show Zetkin as a controversial figure, blamed for dividing both feminist and socialist movements. In addition to contrasting the reception of Zetkin in the two disparate political cultures, Hervé also offers a very useful survey of research devoted to Zetkin on both sides of the historical divide. In conclusion, she traces the historiographical trends since German reunification.

By bringing together these perspectives from four European countries and the SWI on Zetkin's leadership and influence, this collection of essays demonstrates the breadth and depth of her contributions to international socialism. In the final essay, Susan Zimmermann focuses on Zetkin's internationalism and her efforts to use the SWI as a bridge across national borders. Drawing on sources from recently opened East German archives, she shows how Zetkin positioned herself and the SWI in support of leftist politics associated with Rosa Luxemburg on issues of representational politics, global inequality and militarism. Pointing out that Zetkin viewed the 'bourgeois' nation-state as 'the fatherland of the propertied', Zimmermann highlights Zetkin's profound dedication to overcoming nationalist representation and the 'social patriotism' that in her view fed into imperialist wars. In this anti-imperialist stance, Zimmermann shows, the SWI distinguished itself from other women's internationalist movements of the time.

In addition to her leadership of the international socialist women's group – referred to variously as the International Conference of Socialist Women, the Socialist Women's International, the Women's International Council, the International Women's Secretariat – this volume proposes that Zetkin played a significant role in addressing the fundamental questions of class struggle and war and peace that dominated socialist politics in the early twentieth century. While recognising that politics past and present may determine the light in which she is viewed, its authors hope thereby to bring renewed appreciation for Clara Zetkin as one of that world's most dedicated and accomplished leaders.

A young Clara Zetkin

Chapter One

Clara Zetkin and France: Eight Year Exile, Eighty Year Influence[1]

Marilyn J Boxer

Revered in the East, reviled in the West, loved or hated according to ideologies of the Cold War, Clara Zetkin presents the historian seeking to assess her legacy with a complex tapestry of threads to follow. No matter which of the scenes one chooses to weave into her story, it seems important to examine how Zetkin's experience of exile in France affected her political evolution, the development of the socialist women's movement in France, and the French left. As Gilbert Badia and Florence Hervé remind us, in their review of Tânia Puschnerat's recent biography of Zetkin, knowledge of her Paris exile is essential to understanding the mentality and politics of this German 'feminist without borders'. The latter phrase, the title of Badia's biography, would, of course, have been rejected by Zetkin, who refused to accept that label for herself.[2] While considering Zetkin's larger legacy, this chapter will focus primarily on the long-lasting influence of her politics on the French feminist and socialist movements.

Formative years

The facts of Zetkin's life between September 1882, when she arrived in Paris to join Ossip Zetkin, the Russian revolutionary exile who became her partner, and the autumn of 1890, when the expiration of the anti-socialist laws in Germany allowed her to return to her native land, have been recounted many times.[3] These were, it is said, 'the decisive years'. It was in this period that Zetkin lived her self-described proletarian experience.[4] This was constituted of three dimensions: people, politics and poverty. The people of her several socialist circles included native French, German, Polish and Russian émigrés, and a few exiled from other European countries. The politics she experienced included some internal to the French movement, including rivalry between the Parti ouvrier français (French workers' party), the Marxist party of Jules Guesde, Paul and Laura Marx Lafargue (who became close friends of Clara and Ossip), and the Fédération des Travailleurs socialistes de France (Federation of socialist workers of France), the so-called possibiliste party of Paul Brousse, and some external, including confrontations with police, during one of which Zetkin suffered a sword-cut to her foot. The poverty was attendant on the couple's meagre earnings through language lessons and translations, which meant knowing hunger, eating horsemeat, pawning possessions and enduring eviction from their flat for non-payment of rent, which led to a day that Zetkin spent in the street with her two small sons.[5] Overall, however, what Zetkin described as a 'painful life à la bohême' was, in the view of Puschnerat, who attributes to Zetkin a fundamentally 'bourgeois mentality', quite unlike the life of a typical proletarian, and more a kind of 'intellectual Bohême'. At the worst of times, the Zetkins could count on help from other socialist revolutionaries.[6]

It was in France, writing about the French socialist movement and its leaders, that Zetkin launched her career as a socialist, internationalist and journalist. Much of the information about Zetkin's life in Paris, and her observations about French socialism, comes from letters she wrote to Karl Kautsky, editor of the Stuttgart-based socialist journal, *Die Neue Zeit*,-the new time- where in 1886 she published a lengthy biographical essay on Louise Michel in which she portrays Michel, heroine of the Paris Commune, as the revolutionary counterpart of what Zetkin calls the idol of the bourgeois class, Jeanne d'Arc. Zetkin also wrote mini-biographies of other contemporary French socialists of her acquaintance, including Lafargue, Benoît Malon and Edouard Vaillant.[7] Guided by Lafargue, she studied Karl Marx and Friedrich Engels. She visited the Louvre and read Daudet, Maupassant, Zola, Tolstoy, expanding her already considerable knowledge of art and literature. She subscribed to Italian and French workers' journals and read English as well.[8] Marxists speaking a potpourri of European languages gathered at the Zetkin flat, speaking English, both British and American, French, German, Italian, Spanish, Russian, and representing what Zetkin's early biographer, Luise Dornemann, calls 'the great international family of working people'. The Zetkin household hosted a kind of 'salon' for revolutionaries.[9]

Having soon to face her partner's illness and early death from tuberculosis in January 1889, Zetkin's responsibilities for wage-earning and childcare grew. As she learned firsthand the trials of a working single mother, Zetkin also began to write about women's struggles. 'Industry', she declared in *Le Socialiste* in 1887, 'tears women out of the patriarchal foyer to be imprisoned in the jails of [industrialists] and forced to compete with men'.[10] The following month she published a piece on 'Liberté et moralité', charging capitalism with responsibility for the traffic in girls.[11] While caring for Ossip and her sons (born in 1883 and 1885), Zetkin wrote steadily for French, German, Austrian and Swiss journals; Ossip wrote also, and together the pair published more than 300 articles between 1886 and 1890.[12]

International leadership

Chosen by her French colleagues as the German representative on the organising committee for the founding meeting of the Second International in Paris in 1889, Zetkin drew on her studies and her experience to prepare for the famous speech in which she outlined the principles that, somewhat modified, became the position of international socialism on the 'woman question'.[13] Zetkin went on to become the leader of European socialist women, and founder of what American historian Ellen Dubois terms 'arguably the largest international feminist movement ever'.[14] With her facility in languages and familiarity with many revolutionary socialist circles, having lived in Germany, France, Austria and Switzerland, partnered with a Russian, hosted guests from Rumania, Italy, Spain and perhaps elsewhere, Zetkin embodied the international socialism that she pioneered.

Thanks to her maternal ancestry and her 'bourgeois' woman's education in multiple languages, Zetkin often served as translator at international socialist meetings.[15] From her first issue as editor of *Die Gleichheit*, the socialist women's journal founded in December 1890 that she began to edit in January 1892, Zetkin reported on women's movements in other lands.[16] She edited with a heavy hand, emphasising theory and excluding contributors whose views she disapproved of, most notably Lily Braun.[17] As the representative of the Social Democratic Party of Germany (SPD), whose success in organising women was unparalleled, Zetkin won admiration and followers across the world. But it was her hostility to what she labelled 'bourgeois feminism' that was imitated in France and that proved to be perhaps her most lasting contribution to international socialism.[18]

The International Conference of Socialist Women convened by Zetkin (now sometimes called the Socialist Women's International, or SWI) and headquartered at her Stuttgart home, never developed an international bureaucracy.[19] But it did hold two international conferences that attracted an impressive number of delegates – 58 from thirteen countries attended the 1907 conference in Stuttgart, 100 from seventeen countries in 1910 at Copenhagen – and it had important consequences, of which the most enduring is the worldwide celebration of International Women's Day (IWD), initiated at the 1910 meeting on a motion by 'Clara Zetkin, Käte Duncker and other comrades'.[20] A third meeting, planned for August 1914 in Vienna, fell victim to the First World War, though one might consider Zetkin's call to socialist women from belligerent countries to meet in Berne the following March as its substitute. Or as more than that, for Zetkin saw the women's meeting as 'doing the preparatory work for a joint action of the big International'.[21] It also provided an opportunity for Zetkin to depart somewhat from the rigid division of women on grounds of class that she demanded, for she wanted her anti-war appeal to reach out broadly.[22] This 'Extraordinary Socialist Women's Conference' at Berne was followed by a less well-known meeting, an 'Informal Socialist Women's Conference' held at Stockholm in September 1917, in conjunction with the third meeting of socialists from belligerent countries who had first assembled after the women, in Zimmerwald, in September 1915. Yet another international socialist women's meeting, planned for autumn 1919, was never held.[23]

IWD was first celebrated in France in 1914, earning a letter of commendation from Zetkin herself. This 'truly good news', as she put it, elicited a lengthy address from German socialist women to their French 'sisters'. It commanded almost the full front page of the latter's new journal, L'Equité- Equality; and was read aloud at a meeting presided over by Louise Saumoneau the day following the 8 March celebration.[24] But Zetkin's organisation seems to have influenced women and socialism in France rather little. Prior to the war, before Zetkin issued her call to meet in Berne in March 1915 and provided a personal model of resistance to the international conflict by going to jail for her anti-war protests, there are few detailed records of Zetkin's interaction with French socialist and feminist women. But Zetkin followed socialist women's activities in France closely; her name appeared periodically in French socialist journals; and a few encounters were reported.[25]

For example, at the fifth conference of the Second International, held in Paris in late September 1900, two weeks after the important international feminist Congress on the Condition and Rights of Women, Marie Bonnevial, a syndicalist teacher active in socialist and feminist circles, interrupted a speech by Rosa Luxemourg to offer Zetkin a bouquet in appreciation of her contributions as a feminist. Zetkin, doubtless cognisant of the earlier, highly publicised conference, snapped, 'I'm not a feminist, I'm a socialist'. These words brought applause from socialist Charles Vérecque, who, reminiscing about the event in an article reprinted three decades afterwards by Saumoneau, lamented that Zetkin's sharp response, because it was omitted from official records, had been lost to history.[26] Differences also emerged at the 1907 socialist women's conference in Stuttgart where, during a debate over support for woman suffrage independent of men's, Madeleine Pelletier, who favoured it, clashed with Zetkin. The French *doctoresse* also contested Zetkin's insistence on a 'clean break' between women's movements. As war neared, Blanche Echès, writing in *L'Equité* about Zetkin's anti-war appeal, spoke of the 'enormous moral authority' commanded by the German leader. Marianne Rauze credited Zetkin for having brought her to socialism.[27]

French acolyte, Louise Saumoneau

But the greatest influence of Clara Zetkin on relations between French socialism and feminism came through her impact on Louise Saumoneau. Saumoneau, younger than Zetkin by eighteen years, found in the German leader an ideological soulmate and an inspirational role model. Zetkin's apparent success in drawing tens of thousands of women to membership in the SPD, along with her editorship of *Die Gleichheit*, provided her with prestige unequalled among women socialists, none of whom could match her claim to leadership. What Saumoneau could, however, equal, was the level of vituperative rhetoric Zetkin reserved for 'bourgeois' feminists. 'It was this hostility', says historian Charles Sowerwine, 'which French socialist women imitated' – none more than Louise Saumoneau, I would add. Historian Christine Bard couples this pair, Saumoneau and Zetkin, as models of a kind of 'escalated anti-feminism' ['*surenchère antiféministe*'].[28]

    Like her mentor, who refused to participate in any collaborative effort with non-socialist feminists whom she dismissed as 'bourgeois', even against opposition from her German socialist colleagues and party leaders, Saumoneau throughout her long career insisted on a total separation of efforts, despite its price of failure to attract any significant following among French working women. What Sowerwine terms 'the triumph of Louise Saumoneau', referring to her wresting control of the French socialist women's group formed in 1913, also assured Zetkin's continuing influence.[29] During the war, Saumoneau's close adherence to Zetkin's position on class collaboration reappeared in her relations to the mainstream of French socialism when, like Zetkin, she distanced herself from the party leadership that voted to support its bourgeois nationalist government. Responding to Zetkin's November 1914 call in *Die Gleichheit*, to socialist women of all belligerent countries to meet in resistance to the war, and perhaps to a personal request as well, Saumoneau republished the appeal in her journal, *La Femme socialiste,*-The woman socialist - in February 1915.[30] She also helped distribute it throughout Paris and into the provinces.[31] But Saumoneau found herself, in her own socialist women's group, virtually a party of one. After the group voted not to send a delegate to Zetkin's meeting in Berne, Saumoneau ventured across the border to Switzerland alone, *sans passeport*. Resigning from the group, she formed a miniscule one of her own, calling it the Comité d'action féminine socialiste pour la paix contre le chauvinisme (Socialist women's action committee for peace and against chauvinism), and sent a note of congratulations to Zetkin for her leadership Zetkin in turn praised French women for distributing her appeal 'The echo of this courageous action will affirm the desire for peace of the female proletariat in all countries', she wrote.[32]

Like Zetkin, Saumoneau bravely went to jail for her opposition to her country's war effort. Returning from Berne, she pursued a pacifist campaign, distributing thousands of copies of Zetkin's appeal, along with two others of her own authorship. Arrested in early October 1915, she was not released until late November.[33] In the months that followed, Saumoneau's attempts to create a socialist women's group according to her own lights failed, her efforts eclipsed by the war and opposed by women with other views.[34] On the occasion of IWD in 1917, Saumoneau read a letter from Zetkin and spoke of Zetkin's anti-war work and of the German leader's imprisonment, so like her own. And like Zetkin, she would never forgive her party for violating its socialist internationalism to support a war that she saw as serving the interests of capitalism, even to the point, in Saumoneau's case, of refusing its offer of a pension in her last years.[35]

The adherence to socialist internationalism that motivated the two women's anti-war work later carried them both into the successor to the Second International, the Third International

14

founded by Lenin and the Bolsheviks, although Saumoneau adhered only briefly and Zetkin to the end of her life. Writing in April 1919, Saumoneau firmly stated her support for her German role model: 'At the point in revolutionary development where we now stand, I am in full accord with Clara Zetkin'.[36] Retrospectively, however, she would consider her choice to join the Third International a mistake, the 'twenty-one conditions' imposed for adherence as 'murderous', and those who accepted them its 'victims'.[37] Zetkin herself, claimed an unsigned obituary later published in Saumoneau's journal, 'never became an authentic Communist'.[38] Yet Saumoneau, interestingly, was excluded from the Third International not by her own choice but by action of its executive committee, for 'indiscipline'.[39]

Following the war, Saumoneau was not alone in showing support for Zetkin. Writing in *Le Populaire* - The Popular - soon after the Armistice, Marthe Bigot took issue with the ('bourgeois') Conseil national des femmes françaises (National council of French women), which had refused to respond to an initiative from German women asking for a softening of the conditions of armistice. Placing French women socialists alongside the British, she called for all to 'affirm their international solidarity to Clara Zetkin [...]. We are with Clara Zetkin and Rosa Luxemburg and Louise Zietz and Bertha Thalheimer who cry out against the crime of their government, at the peril of their liberty and even their life'. Bigot presented her readers with the text of Zetkin's call for a new meeting of international women socialists to formulate proposals for peace negotiations that would include rights for women workers and mothers. The following month another Frenchwoman, Monette Thomas, pursued the topic of Zetkin's appeal.[40]

Dividing French socialism

From an early date, Zetkin enjoyed a special relationship with French socialists, for many of whom she had served as translator at international meetings. It was a relationship that overcame French reservations about Germans.[41] Zetkin's wartime condemnation of her government and of her party's support of it, earned her the admiration of French socialists, which they demonstrated in the thunderous applause that greeted her unexpected appearance at the crucial postwar meeting of the SFIO (French section of the workers' international) at Tours in the last week of December 1920. The purpose of this famous meeting was to decide the party's future:

whether to discard the old Second International, discredited by its failure to adhere to its internationalist, anti-war principles, and to join the new Third International of Lenin and the Bolsheviks, who, in contrast, were enhanced and emboldened by their victorious revolution. Earlier in the day a long letter from Zetkin had been read to the congress, lamenting her absence, which was due, she wrote, to her inability to obtain permission from French authorities to cross the border. Now, suddenly, the ageing but stalwart German socialist stood there, returning to France to be greeted as a hero by the 370 delegates, including about a dozen women. With the opening words of his 1993 biography, Gilbert Badia takes us back to that event:

> Congress of Tours. Tuesday, 28 December 1920. Marcel Sembat presides. Since early afternoon, L.O. Frossard speaks. Suddenly an interruption. The lights dim. A shiver runs through the assembly. A few seconds later, when the lights go up, a woman with almost white hair stands at the dais. A woman whom the congress, which rises as one, acclaims: it is Clara Zetkin, the delegate of the Third International, saluted by the session leader with these words: 'This great, noble, and glorious woman who, with her glorious friends, Karl Liebknecht and Rosa Luxemburg, was the ardent and magnificent soul of the German Revolution.'[42]

Reported two days later in *Le Populaire* as a 'coup de théâtre', Zetkin's intervention urged the delegates to cast away their allegiance to the failed internationalism of the Second International and to embrace the hopes of the Third, accepting the harsh twenty-one conditions imposed by the Bolshevik leaders.[43] 'I urge you', she proclaimed, 'to split your [national] party to achieve a more precious [international] unity'. They should eliminate all 'social patriots and vacillating centrists, and form a single revolutionary force capable of disciplined vigorous action', she advised. 'Who is not with us, in this revolutionary era, is against us'. Described by French historian-activist Annie Kriegel as 'moving, noble, eloquent', her twenty-minute speech ended with the cry, 'Vive la Révolution proletarienne, which will destroy the capitalist world and give free access to the coming of our Communism'.[44] Then, departing as quickly as she had arrived, Zetkin disappeared. To prevent any 'spy' from following her trail, the doors were locked.

In the view of *Le Populaire*, Zetkin 'pronounced the words that ended the last hesitation'. After two more days of debate, which included several references to the words of 'our revered Clara Zetkin', the delegates voted overwhelmingly to go forward with the new International. Zetkin's presence had 'added considerable emotional weight' to the Third International's position, recalled Rappoport.[45] The dramatic events won attention around the world. 'Mocking the police ['A la barbe de la police'], Clara Zetkin arrives at Tours', headlined *L'Humanité* the following day, 29 December. The *New York Times,* announcing 'German Woman Fires French Reds', emphasised the clandestine aspect of Zetkin's trip, and the locked doors and severed telegraph wires in the assembly hall. Another *Times* article noted that the incident elicited an apology from the French government for the well-known socialist's success in eluding authorities at the border. Following 'pandemonium' in the Chamber during discussion of Zetkin's triumph, however, the government won a strong vote of confidence. The report in *Le Populaire* stressed the impact on the congress of her sudden appearance, describing how 'the entire assembly, from the right to the left, rose up to sing the revolutionary anthem, whose words could barely emerge from throats choked with emotion'. Commenting on Zetkin's youthfulness and passion, they declaimed, 'C'est le Bolshevisme itself which stands there'.[46] It was Bolshevism with a familiar, friendly face; Zetkin's intervention seems to have countered the hostile reception given to the more famous telegram of Zinoviev.[47]

Afterlife in postwar France

While Tours may have marked the last of Zetkin's personal presence in France, it seems only to have enhanced her influence on Saumoneau, who followed her mentor into the Third International and sought to bring others with her. Quoting Zetkin on the 'decomposition of the old social democracy', Saumoneau wrote articles denigrating the Second International and offered her readers long quotations from Zetkin and Zetkin's new journal, *Die Kommunistin* - The woman communist.[48] For her efforts, she was listed, along with Zetkin and three other eminent socialist women – Angelica Balabanova, Henrietta Roland Holst and Sylvia Pankhurst – on the masthead of *The Communist International*, the official organ of the Third International.[49]

Thanks to Saumoneau's political longevity, and to her predilection for republishing old news in her long-lived journal, *La Femme socialiste*, ideas from the pre-war and wartime eras, along with reprinted texts, continued to appear in France for several decades. Saumoneau also attempted to revive institutions from the earlier period. In 1923 she declared her desire to re-establish the SWI, whose agenda, she now envisioned, would include numerous women's, indeed feminist, issues, such as the rights of mothers and children and paternity claims. While Saumoneau's reputedly vexatious personality and her intransigence on many issues tended to alienate rather than attract followers, nevertheless, her anti-war activity won her admiration and access to leadership positions in the reconstituted SFIO, which Saumoneau rejoined after her expulsion from the Third International, including membership on its administrative committee.

In this renewed party, 'one woman would stand out above all others', states Sowerwine, and that was Louise Saumoneau.[50] In March 1922, she called on the remaining members of the pre-war organisation of socialist women to form a new group, reconstructed with the same constraints as the old; that is, open only to women who were already members of the socialist party. The new group adopted her journal as its own. In 1924 it elected Saumoneau to her old position as secretary, a role she continued to fill until 1930. Her policy of requiring prior membership in the party and her adamant resistance to any 'feminist' influence lived on, continuing to stymie efforts to increase the group's numbers. Even in the mid-1930s, when feminist groups called for a 'women's world rally' against fascism, it turned its back. It also failed to advance the cause of women's political rights by demanding the vote, even during the socialist-led Popular Front of that period.[51] The male-led party might collaborate to form a government; but the women, led by Saumoneau, would disdain any form of cross-class collaboration. Resurrecting pre-war politics, Saumoneau's influence lived on into the 1970s. As Christine Bard has put it, 'saumonisme' prevailed.[52] It embodied the spirit of Zetkin.

Zetkin's career following her dramatic intervention at Tours transpired in Germany and the Soviet Union, where she lived for many years, fulfilling a ceremonial role but also active as a travelling propagandist and leader in workers' relief efforts, until her death there in June 1933. This period of Zetkin's life, ending with what she complained of as 'solitary confinement', offers less of interest to the historian of France and of feminism than does the journey of her ideas across time and space.[53] Elsewhere I have traced what I call the 'international career of the concept "bourgeois feminism"' that she did so much to construct and to promulgate.[54] In my view,

Zetkin's success in this endeavour represents the most broadly influential part of her legacy.

Assessing a legacy

Symbolically, of course, Zetkin lived on, loved and lionised in many parts of the Soviet Union, where parks, schools, streets and all manner of public facilities bear her name. Scarcely recognised in the West, she was restored to our history during the 1970s by pioneering historians of women, including British historians Richard J Evans and Sheila Rowbotham, and American historians of women, several of whom wrote dissertations on Zetkin and German social democracy between 1964 and 1976. She reappeared as well in the socialist-influenced medium of women's studies programmes that burgeoned in the USA and spread across Western Europe during the 1970s and 1980s. In these programmes, course readings often featured selections from Marxist writings that included excerpts from Zetkin, mostly taken from her famous 1920 interview about women's issues with Lenin (who, like Zetkin, castigated non-socialist feminism).[55] Disdain for feminism likewise reappeared and was especially strong in France, where a 'radical anti-bourgeois bias' prevailed among intellectuals.[56] But its creator, Clara Zetkin, remained little known, as Badia emphasises in his 1993 biography. '[W]ho then in France today – apart from a few historians knows that Zetkin was, in Europe and perhaps in the world, in the years that preceded the First World War the most famous woman socialist?'[57]

Furthermore, little work has appeared about the international group of socialist women that Zetkin created. Its history, like hers, has suffered from the division she did so much to create and to perpetuate. The lack of unity among those who work to improve women's lot and lives, the refusal of coalition building across class and ideological divides, have hindered the progress of women's movements.[58] It is hard for some of us whom Zetkin would have dismissed as 'bourgeois feminists' – whatever our true class experience – to love Clara.

Once you get to know her, however, you must admire her: for her learning, for her courage, and for her dedication to improve women's lives, albeit in her own way, and for socialist purposes; for her early and steadfast commitment to anti-war and anti-fascist causes; and, as Badia, writing after the opening of archives in Eastern Europe, proposes, for her attempts at resistance to Bolshevik dictates. Puschnerat agrees that Zetkin never fully supported

Bolshevisation, although as a 'typical Comintern diplomat and party bureaucrat', she became a good 'party soldier'.[59] Zetkin was an inspirational figure, and for some, she remains so.[60] She represented for many on the left the best hopes for a just and peaceful world. For Charles Rappoport she served as a 'beam of socialist light'. For the French poet Louis Aragon, she embodied the woman of modern times who is no longer subservient, man's equal in a world beyond war. Aragon's 'new woman' was a socialist, named Clara. 'It is of her that I shall sing', he concluded his novel, *The Bells of Basel*, which is named for the international socialist congress of 1912 held in that city, where Zetkin first gave her anti-war appeal to the mothers of all nations.[61]

But what of her legacy? Starting with her July 1889 speech in Paris at the founding meeting of the Second International, Zetkin deserves credit for bringing the 'woman question' as an issue, and perhaps also women as individuals, to the attention of the Second International. She stressed the contributions of women to revolutions past and insisted their participation was vital to socialist revolution in the future. This marked a major advance over attitudes expressed toward women by its predecessor association, the First International led by Karl Marx.[62] But Zetkin failed to get socialist parties to adopt any real women's programme. And the theory that she developed about feminism served women ill. Some have argued that her ideas changed over time, and she seems to have encouraged class collaboration in combating war. But she never relented in emphasising the class divide. In 1914 she wrote, 'Since Copenhagen the development of things has shown in an unequivocal fashion the dangerous and reactionary character of limited suffrage for women. It has destroyed the last illusions about what bourgeois suffragists could pursue in common with proletarian socialist women'.[63] A decade later, writing to Fanny Jezierska about IWD, she insisted that women's claims be subsumed into demands for the working classes.[64]

Zetkin's most lasting legacy was – and arguably still is – the invention and reification of the concept 'bourgeois feminism', with its straw woman who allegedly cares only for the interests of women of the dominant classes. This construction is belied by all that women of the educated and/or prosperous classes – the much maligned 'bourgeoises' – have done to improve the lives of those of their sex less favoured by family and fortune. Many feminist movements grew out of such efforts. By emphasising what divides women of differing backgrounds or politics, and eclipsing what may serve to unite them, Zetkin served women of all classes poorly. Through her acolyte Louise Saumoneau, Zetkin's views on feminism retained their currency in France for many decades. Her influence on French socialism likewise fostered division. How her dramatic intervention at Tours, and whatever backstage politics accompanied it, really affected voting behaviour is uncertain. But the result in both cases was to foster divides that in the long run harmed the women's and working-class movements to which Clara Zetkin devoted her life and her work. She preached division, she sowed division. Little wonder that assessments of her legacy stand sharply divided and that she is both loved and hated today. She can also be viewed as a tragic figure who saw her beloved revolution perverted. Historians of women may wish to honour Zetkin, especially in recognising the recent centennial of IWD. But we must also acknowledge the deep ambivalence of her legacy.

Statue in Clara Zetkin Park, Leipzig

Chapter Two

International Socialist Women's Secretary in Wartime: Clara Zetkin and Britain, 1912-1915[1]

John S Partington

Although it is often written that the outbreak of the First World War in August 1914 came as a surprise to the vast majority of people, many political thinkers and activists had nonetheless been warning about and preparing for a general European conflagration for many years before. Within the Second International, international wars and imperial conflicts were the subjects of condemnation throughout its worldwide membership from its foundation in 1889. At its 1912 congress in Basle the Second International combined its anti-war principle with practical action, starting a momentum which, for a small cadre of the Second International at least, would continue with the outbreak of the First World War.

In what follows, I will focus on the leadership activities of Clara Zetkin at the two socialist peace congresses of 1912 and 1915 as gleaned from the pages of the British socialist and labour press.[2] During that period Zetkin was the secretary of the Socialist Women's International (SWI) and as such was the focal point for many anti-war socialist women in Britain. Not only was she the international leader of the socialist and labour women, but as an anti-militarist leader in enemy Germany, she represented the voice of sanity during a time of international crisis, living proof that comradeship could traverse battlefronts.

Although Zetkin concentrated her efforts at uniting socialist women around the cause of peace, the failure of the pro-war and anti-war factions of the Second International to resolve their differences between 1914 and 1919 led to a leftwing secession from the democratic socialist movement. What emerged after the First World War was a more ideologically concentrated international communist movement which made anti-militarism its byword, but which also drifted away from the democratic socialist movement following perceived betrayals of socialism by the Second International between 1917 and 1919.[3] From her efforts to unite socialist women, Zetkin ultimately joined the small leftwing group of comrades in founding the Communist Party of Germany (KPD), and ended her career as the leader of the international communist women's movement of the Third International.

Background: Clara Zetkin and 'war against war'

Clara Zetkin was a true stalwart of the Second International. Having been present and active at its founding congress in 1889, she attended every one of its gatherings and even founded the SWI in 1907. Zetkin positioned herself on the left of the socialist movement, rejecting reformism in favour of orthodox Marxism and arguing for working class mobilisation to defeat threats posed by bourgeois society. While issues such as education and universal adult suffrage absorbed much of her energy, propagating anti-war sentiments was also a crucial plank in her politics.

It was during the Second Boer War (1899-1902) that Zetkin expressed her anti-war position in Britain for the first time.[4] In a 1900 May Day greeting from the Social Democratic Party of Germany (SPD) to its British counterpart, the Social Democratic Federation (SDF), published in *Justice*, Zetkin writes, the SDF's 'manly attitude during this deplorable war against the Boers, brought about by the sordid and unscrupulous greed of a small number of gold-hunters, stock-jobbers and adventurers, will be one of the purest glories in the history of Socialism', and she asserts that,

> Wherever on the first of May the working class cries to capitalist society: 'Peace on earth! Fraternity between the nations! War against war!' their thoughts and sympathies will turn towards that gallant little body of Socialist fighters in England, which dares to oppose the Socialist ideals and revendications to a world of power, of prejudice and of misled passions, roused by the present criminal war.[5]

Although anti-imperialism would be enshrined in the policy of the Second International from 1904, during the Second Boer War British socialists were divided, with some Fabians and social democrats supporting it, so Zetkin's statement reveals both her own anti-imperialism and her efforts to influence comrades abroad.[6] Zetkin's key phrase is 'war against war' – a call to action rather than a passive opposition – which would appear again and again in her writings and speeches throughout her career.[7]

The Extraordinary International Socialist Congress, Basle, 24 to 25 November 1912

Her condemnation of the Boer War notwithstanding, Zetkin's efforts to mobilise an anti-war movement within international socialism, and especially within the socialist women's movement, began in earnest in 1912 as Balkan tensions erupted into a regional war which many feared might turn into a general European conflagration. The First Balkan War broke out on 8 October 1912 in a struggle between the Balkan League (Bulgaria, Greece, Montenegro and Serbia) and the Ottoman Empire. The Balkans was a field of international power politics, with Russia, Austria-Hungary and the Ottoman Empire seeking to maintain and increase their respective influences in the region, while Germany, France and Britain remained in the wings, anxious to ensure a balance of power in their individual favours.

Recognising the wider threat posed by the war in the Balkans, the International Socialist Bureau (ISB) responded by calling an Extraordinary International Socialist Congress in Basle from 24 to 25 November.[8] It is suggestive of the urgency of the situation that the ISB organised the congress with a minimum of notice. Zetkin wrote the appeal for delegates in Britain, publishing her first letter on the subject in the *Daily Herald* on 19 November, just five days before the congress convened, following this up with letters to the *Labour Leader* and *The Clarion*, while *Justice* quoted her appeal in its pages and the *League Leaflet*, a monthly, reported it retrospectively.[9]

Zetkin begins her appeal by warning that 'the atrocious war in the Balkans will be surpassed by the much greater horrors of a universal war between the great European States' if the proletariat does not act. She then goes on to give two reasons why it is in the interests of the masses to oppose such a general war: firstly, it would be 'disastrous for the working classes as well as for their gigantic struggle to overthrow capitalism and to open the way to Socialism and the higher evolution of humanity', and secondly, to protect 'civilisation, which is threatened by the iron foot and ensanguined hand of International war'.[10]

While opposition to proletarians fighting proletarians was well grounded in socialist thought by 1912, and the notion that the 'struggle against war will strike a mortal blow to capitalism, and peace will show the way to Socialism' were commonplace rhetorical assertions, Zetkin's concern for the protection of 'civilisation' moves her anti-militarism beyond the narrow realms of political ideology, infusing it with a gendered argument. For Zetkin, civilisation did not represent the cultural achievements of an educated elite, but was manifested in women's biological function, as 'they look on civilisation as a precious heirloom to be handed on to future generations'. In Zetkin's account, the loss of their menfolk makes women victims of war, as the 'blood that is to drench the fields of battle is that of their sons, husbands and brothers. Women who have worked and wept refuse to give up their loved ones to be shamelessly and callously slaughtered through the frenzy of the military and Imperialist factions'.[11]

Having organised international socialist women's conferences that met ahead of the previous two international socialist congresses (in 1907 and 1910), Zetkin regrets that it will not be possible to send a number of women delegates to Basle 'commensurate with the great interest taken by women in safeguarding peace and proportionate to the importance of the collaboration and assistance of women in the fight against Imperialism and war'. She asserts that it 'is, therefore, urgent that our male comrades should give their help in securing the presence of women delegates to the Congress'. This would both ensure a role for women in the congress, but also 'show that in all countries Socialist women are united with the workers and the Socialist Parties in waging war against war'.[12]

In addition to inviting delegates to Basle, Zetkin's role in the congress also received coverage in Britain. Thus, Dora Montefiore mentions walking between Zetkin and Rosa Luxemburg during the congress's Sunday demonstration and,

> On hearing about the compulsory military training of all Australian and New Zealand boys over 12 years of age, Clara Zetkin arranged an evening meeting in one of the large halls in Basle in order that I might put before an international audience these facts of military preparation on the part of the British Empire, which, though known to European and other Governments, were not generally known among the people.[13]

In the *Labour Leader* Keir Hardie, the Labour MP and Independent Labour Party (ILP) delegate to Basle, in his report of the congress, observes that 'Klara Zetkin, happily recovered after a long and severe illness, was hailed with delight when she appeared on the Forum' and Mary Macpherson in the *League Leaflet* notes that 'Comrade Zetkin as the Secretary of the Women's International

Council, was unanimously chosen to voice a strong protest against war in the name of the Socialist women of all countries'.[14]

The most comprehensive coverage of Zetkin's role at the congress, however, came in an article in *Justice* entitled 'Socialist Women and the International Demonstration at Basel'. The article notes that Zetkin was nominated by the socialist women of all countries to present the following declaration at the congress: 'The women, the mothers, of the labouring masses are prepared for the most untiring and dangerous war against war, and are ready to give their whole strength for freedom and for Socialism'. The article also notes Zetkin's appearance, along with Montefiore and others, at a meeting convened by the Basle Women Workers' Association, chaired by Ida Schmidt, 'from which hundreds had to be turned away'.[15]

Zetkin's major role, however, came with her speech to the congress where she elaborates on the special concerns socialist women have on the issue of war and peace. Her growing emphasis on the maternal function and the female body as the conduit of civilisation becomes more explicit in the speech, declaring as she does that, 'with our sex throughout all the ages has gone the function of bearing, nourishing and rearing new human life. [...] All that is within us as the personal expression of general human development, general ideas of culture, is revolted at the thought of the threatening wholesale destruction of human life in modern warfare'.[16] Zetkin sees socialist women as responsible both for the protection of their offspring from capitalist exploitation, including war, as well as for raising the next generation of soldiers of social-ism, fighting capitalism and – if needs be – dying for the revolution. Thus, she asserts, 'we will not hesitate to see our loved ones fight and fall if it be for the cause of freedom. In that struggle we will be filled with the spirit of those mothers of old who handed the shield to their sons with the words: "Return either with it or upon it"'.[17] She concluded her speech with the words of Friedrich Schiller: 'And if you do not risk your life,/You will never win life'.[18]

If the Basle congress cannot be considered responsible for preventing a general European war, it certainly focussed socialists' attention on the issue of anti-militarism, and demonstrated the potential mobilisation of anti-war activity across Europe. In Britain, inspired by the congress, the Annual Report of the British Section of the Women's International Council of Socialist and Labour Or-ganisations, published in November 1913, reported the participation of the Council at a conference on 'War against war', initiated by the ILP. As a result of the conference, the Council became 'actively engaged in preparing for a campaign against militarism' and announced the preparation of 'a Leaflet on war from women's point of view, which is to contain a message from German women'.[19] In addition, the Council planned a working women's peace visit to Germany for early 1914.[20] In December 1913 the said 'message from German women', written by Zetkin, was published in *Labour Woman*, though its publication as a leaflet was not pursued.[21]

Zetkin's message is clearly inspired by 'the recent wars in the Balkans' and the fear that 'a gigantic war [...] which not yet has happened, may happen one day' between 'the Great European States'. From the start, her message is defensive, reassuring her comrades in Britain of the solidarity of the German working women who 'have strongly the feeling that at this very moment they must send you a message of peace, fraternity and freedom'. Of the ruling classes she observes: 'To keep the people willing to pay with goods and with blood the sacrifices of armaments and war, they talk always so there shall be hostility and hatred between the nations'.[22] In response Zetkin asserts:

> We do not believe the stories that certain German newspapers and politicians tell us about the jealousy and the ferocious animosity of the British against our people. [...] And we entreat you most earnestly not to take it as truth what certain English Newspapers and politicians tell you of the feelings of the people of Germany. We emphasize, *they are not true* [...]; it is a deceitful story with which half a dozen fanatic German jingoes abuse our papers and patience.[23]

In addition to attacking the media and politicians for stirring up international antagonism, Zetkin is also critical of the ruling classes for using war as a tool of class oppression and exploitation. Of the government she writes:

> They waste the money which they take out of the working people's pockets in building barracks and Dreadnoughts; in buying field-artillery, naval-guns, and all the most perfect instruments and means of mass-murder and mass-devastation on land, on sea, and even in the air; in drilling thousands and thousands of young workers to be one day the Cains of their brethren abroad.[24]

Regarding the capitalists, she scorns,

the powerful directors, and share-holders of military and naval arsenals, the 'kings' of gun, armour-plate, smokeless powder and aeroplane production [...] the small number of privileged ones, who pocket enormous profits, thanks to the fantastic expenditure on military and naval armaments, who fish guineas out of the blood-streams on the battlefields, and pluck their laurels from land fertilised by rotting corpses.[25]

Against the media, government and capitalists of Germany, Zetkin offers the proletariat, and especially socialist women, again identifying women's special suffering in times of war. Reflecting on the Balkan Wars, she writes: '[I]n our ears ring the painful sighs and the mad cries coming from waves of mutilated and dying men, thrown side by side with corpses and torn limbs; we hear the sobbing of wives and sisters, of mothers and children, bereaved of their beloved ones and bread-winners'. She asserts the centrality of women's struggle in the fight against war: 'Together with our husbands, sons and brothers we stand for peace and for fraternity between the workers of all countries. Together with them we fight against Capitalism and for Socialism'. Looking ahead, she takes comfort from the fact that 'our children, nourished on the Socialist faith, will finish the work we began and will triumph where we have fought'.[26]

Extraordinary International Conference of Labour and Socialist Women, Berne, 26 to 28 March 1915

If the Balkan Wars were successfully contained, it was not long before a general European conflict broke out in the form of the First World War. Socialist internationalism famously collapsed in August 1914 as the leading leftwing parties in Britain, Germany, France and Austria-Hungary signed up to political truces and allowed their leading members to join coalition governments. Socialist internationalists did not disappear; it simply took time for them to develop an audible language of opposition to the war upon which activism could be built.

Although Zetkin continued to be reported in the British socialist press following the outbreak of the First World War, it was on 17 December 1914 that she made 'An Appeal to the Socialist Women of All Countries'. The appeal was originally published in Zetkin's own journal, *Die Gleichheit*, before being smuggled into Switzerland and sent to Britain where it was reprinted in *Justice*. In her appeal Zetkin condemned the war as 'a war of capitalist conquest and world domination' and she urged: 'If men must kill, it is we women who must fight for life. If men remain silent, it is our duty to speak out'.[27]

With international socialist solidarity re-emerging in the first few months of 1915, Zetkin decided not to wait for the ISB to organise international action for peace. Instead, in the name of the international socialist women, she made arrangements for a conference to be held in Berne, Switzerland, from 26 to 28 March, at which four British delegates were present: Mary Longman, Marion Phillips, Ada Salter and Margaret Bondfield.[28] In fact, there is some suggestion that it was British interest which made the event possible.

In *Labour Woman* for March 1915, Longman reported that 'The letters we have lately received from abroad all discuss the possibility of an International Conference of Socialist Women shortly meeting in some neutral country'.[29] Longman, on behalf of the British section of the SWI, wrote that 'We much wish that this hope may be realised', though acknowledging that 'there are certain vexed questions which it would be necessary to avoid' in order to 'come together and discuss what we can do to bring about a just and lasting peace'.[30] Events moved swiftly and in the April issue of *Labour Woman* the conference is reported as 'an accomplished fact' with British women playing no small part.[31] In a letter received by the British section of the SWI, 'Clara Zetkin tells us of the joy with which she received a message from the British women, expressing the hope that a meeting would take place. It came (she said) "like a sunbeam at night"'.[32]

The Berne conference is first reported in an article entitled 'Women's War Against War' in *Labour Woman* in which 'We are at last able to declare the restoration of the Women's International, and to outline the future work for peace to which we are called'. Although the article covers one and a half pages, it is largely a celebration of female solidarity, as '[i]n this issue of the *Labour Woman* we can only deal with the beginnings of the new peace effort, for the matter is being worked out as we write', though 'it is hoped that one result will be the drafting of a manifesto to the women of all countries in popular form, and adapted for distribution as a leaflet'.[33] The conference demonstrated that socialist women retained 'the same sisterly fidelity as of old in the spirit of solidarity and comradeship'.[34]

On 8 April the *Labour Leader* reported the conference, credited to Zetkin's organisation, with 28 delegates in attendance from eight countries.[35] As with *Labour Woman*, the *Labour Leader* states, 'It is impossible as yet to give a full account of the discussions' but 'its proceedings were characterised by great unanimity [and] an official report is being prepared'. The conference reiterated the resolutions passed at earlier international socialist congresses and it 'called for a speedy ending of the war by a peace which will expiate the wrong done to Belgium, impose no humiliating conditions on any nation, and will recognise the right of all nationalities, small and large, to independence and self-government'.[36] The British delegation managed to insert two additions to the first draft of the conference declaration; one dealing with 'the menace of the armament interests and their huge international organisation' and a second dealing with 'the high prices charged for food and fuel, and the extortions of contractors'. The declaration points out that 'the workers are being plundered both in the enhanced prices that they have to pay for their own living, and through taxation, in order to pay the profits that are made by the contractors'. In addition, 'the Conference passed a resolution of sympathy with the International Congress of Women which is to be held at The Hague at the end of this month, declaring that [...] the organised Socialist and Labour women of the different countries welcome any movement which makes for peace'.[37] The report ended by announcing that a conference manifesto was in preparation and would be published shortly.

Coverage of the Berne conference also occurred in *The Herald* on 10 April under the heading 'Women and Peace', an article heavily reliant on content from the *Labour Leader*, though with some additional comments. *The Herald* noted that, although wartime peace conferences had been held in Copenhagen and London prior to the Berne gathering, the women's event was the first to include representatives from across the battlefronts as well as neutrals, and 'British, German, French, and Russian met in friendly sympathy, and the cordial relations between the representatives of Great Britain and Germany were especially marked'.[38]

Continuing its coverage of the Berne conference, the *Labour Leader* was the first journal to report its joint declaration. Although the declaration was agreed to by all attendees, there is clear evidence of Zetkin's hand in much of its wording. As with her prewar utterances, it emphasises the detrimental effects the war was having on humanity's accumulated culture:

> Invaluable gifts of civilisation have been annihilated. The war has raised barriers of barbarism across the path of

progress towards man's highest ideals. [...] At the end of it the nations will be drained of their vital forces, their economic resources will be exhausted, and their social progress indefinitely retarded. [...] Calumnies and insults dishonour each nation, and hide the gifts which each has given to the common civilisation of the world.[39]

For the first time since hostilities began, explicit reference is made to the international war interrupting the class struggle, as 'In place of the war waged by the workers to raise their conditions and to secure their emancipation, is placed the "national truce." International fratricide takes the place of the international solidarity of the workers of the world'. The war is seen as a channel for collective energy: 'The worker's love of country is used to impel him to pour out his energy, self-sacrifice, and valour, not to gain his own emancipation, but to secure the triumph of Capitalist Imperialism'.[40] The ruling class thus exploits the proletariat's patriotism both to strengthen capitalism and to weaken the socialist movement.

In opposition to the capitalist imperialist aims of the warring powers, the declaration sets out demands aimed at healing the divisions in Europe and preventing a recurrence of conflict thereafter: 'Peace without annexations or conquest', a recognition of 'the right of peoples and nations, both large and small, to independence and self-government', 'no humiliating and insupportable conditions upon any country' and 'expiation of the wrong inflicted upon Belgium'. Such a peace was crucial 'in order that [...] the Socialist and Labour organisations may assume their task as the conscious vanguard of progress, gathering and uniting the masses in a solid phalanx round the flag of International Socialism'. By overcoming the many obstacles in the way of their international conference, the declaration heralds women as the vanguard of socialist reconciliation, declaring that 'Such action of Socialist women is the forerunner of the general movement of the workers to bring an end to fratricide, the first step in rebuilding the one great association of the workers'. 'War on this war' is declared 'the holiest duty of Socialist and Labour women'.[41]

With the conference manifesto still not hammered out by May, momentum was maintained through the publication of Marion Phillips's six-page report of the conference, presented as 'A May Message to the Working Women of All Lands' in *Labour Woman*.[42] Phillips begins her report by presenting the resolutions. The primary resolution, which, 'with few alterations and additions had been originally drawn up by the International Secretary, in consultation with the Dutch Socialist women, and submitted to the British section before the Conference met', was the peace declaration.[43] It begins by identifying the root of the war 'in the imperialist ideas of a capitalist society', with the possessing classes seeking to 'strengthen their power by extending their dominion, not only over the workers in their own countries, but also beyond the frontiers of their own nations'.[44] The resolution identifies the power of 'financial interests', and especially the 'great industry of armament making', as controlling nations, causing thousands of deaths and raising 'barriers of barbarism across the path of progress towards man's highest ideals'.[45] It warns of the loss of national vitality and economic resources, and the retardation of social progress. The solidarity of workers with their masters is lamented as preventing 'the war waged by the workers to raise their conditions and to secure their emancipation'.[46] In opposition to the war of conquest, the Berne conference demanded 'War on this war [...] and a peace without annexation or conquest', universal rights to national independence and self-government, and no punitive peace terms.[47]

The resolution was accepted unanimously, but not before a debate on a Bolshevik counter-resolution moved by 'the Russian delegation representing the Organisations of Socialist Women affiliated to the Central Committees [...] supported by the Polish delegate' who together offered an alternative, revolutionary resolution.[48] The counter-resolution,

> condemned all the individuals and parties which had supported the war or had joined capitalist governments. [...] [I]t urged that peace propaganda should be revolutionary in character and called upon the organisations of working women in the different countries represented to form illegal associations to forward such revolutionary action.[49]

On the initiative of the British delegation, the counter-resolution was dismissed on the basis that analysing the socialist split throughout Europe was the task for each socialist movement and one that should take place after the war, while the notion of revolutionary propaganda and illegal activity was deemed inappropriate on the basis that, 'What is revolutionary in one country is not in another' and in some countries, where peace propaganda is legal, 'we do not see the advantage of endeavouring to break the law'.[50]

In addition to the peace resolution, the British delegation sponsored a resolution on prices and wages which condemned capitalists and governments who 'exploit the needs of the people (1) by artificially raising the price of food and other necessaries, (2) by charging enormous prices for the contracts they make with the Governments at war for war materials, [and] (3) by worsening the conditions of labour and the wages of the workers they employ'.51 The resolution concluded by calling 'upon the organised workers to blind themselves no longer by the false notion of a "national truce," and to pursue with vigour their struggle for industrial freedom' and was carried unanimously.52

Reflecting the British tradition of gender solidarity, the final resolution, tabled by the British, 'gladly welcomes all efforts on [sic] non-Socialist organisations in the cause of peace, and recognises the courageous efforts with which the non-Socialist pacificists put forward the ideals of cosmopolitanism against war and national jingoism'. With the resolution's success, Phillips observes that it 'marks a great widening of view amongst Social Democrats, who from the position in which their politics have placed them in continental countries has been usually very reluctant to express any opinion or take any part in the work of non-socialist bodies'. Phillips hoped that the mood expressed by the resolution 'may well point to a general widening of sympathy between those who represent different phases of thought amongst women in the future'.53

In June 1915, *Labour Woman* published the long awaited manifesto as produced by the Berne conference. Unlike the resolutions, which were clearly aimed at activist organisations, the manifesto was intended for the general public, and it was quickly issued as a leaflet for mass distribution. The manifesto highlights the recent international solidarity of the conference, before suggesting in powerful terms why peace has become imperative. In the first place, it unmasks the bogus class solidarity as expressed in the 'national truce':

> You were told of a great brotherhood and sisterhood between high and low, of a truce between rich and poor. Now the truce is seen in the way the merchants and conscienceless speculators raise prices, the employers press down your wages, and the landlord threatens to put you on the streets.54

Secondly, it reveals the suffering of the masses with few or no benefits, current or prospective, to show for it: 'Relief funds are doled out in a niggardly manner, and middle class philanthropy tells you how to cook "poor man's soup"', women suffer 'gnawing anxiety and misery at home' and '[t]he sons that you bore in pain and suffering, that you nourished in cares and sorrows, your comrades in the hard struggle of life, these the war snatches from you'. According to the manifesto, the war was manufactured by the capitalists of all lands: 'For the sake of their profits they have engendered fear and hate between the nations, and so contributed to the outbreak of war'. Using the Berne delegates as examples to the masses, the manifesto exhorts: 'Just as their wills met right across the battlefields, so must you also join together in all lands to raise the one cry, "Peace, Peace!" [...] The workers of all lands are one people of brothers. Only the united will of this people can end war. Socialism alone will bring lasting peace to mankind!'[55]

Conclusion

As her role in propagating 'war against war' from 1900 on reveals, Zetkin self-consciously led the women's anti-militarist campaign within the Second International, and given the extensive coverage in the leftwing press, her leadership was duly acknowledged by British socialists. Although the Berne conference was the last forum in which Zetkin fraternised and organised with British socialists during the First World War, her acknowledgement of the importance of such events is reflected in the fact that she mooted two further gatherings through the pages of the British press.[56]

With the meeting of the Berne conference, and its resultant resolutions and manifesto, world socialism would never be the same again. By 1916 in Britain and 1917 in Germany, the fissures in the socialist movement which would ultimately lead to separate communist and social democratic camps had formed. Zetkin's principled stance on 'war against war' was a major contribution to this split, and one which would see her leaving the SPD in 1917 and becoming a founding member of the KPD in 1919.[57] From December 1914 on Zetkin had declared the need for a successor to the failed Second International and looked forward to the day when 'the third International shall rise';[58] not only did she live to see that day, but she ultimately emerged as the leader of the communist women's movement within the Third International, continuing her call for a 'war against war'[59] until the end of her life, and titling her last published (English-language) book *The Toilers Against War*[60] – a title which could be applied to Zetkin herself as readily as to any other socialist anti-militarist.

Chapter Three

Clara Zetkin and Russia, 1900s-1930s

Natalia Novikova

Clara Zetkin was enormously popular in revolutionary Russia. Streets in many cities, public libraries, colleges and schools, collective farms, maternity hospitals all over Russia were named after this 'leader of the International Socialist Women's Movement'.[1] Today International Woman's Day (IWD), 8 March, remains associated with Zetkin and many Russians only remember her as the founder of this public holiday.

In the 1910s and 1920s, some of Zetkin's texts were translated into Russian, but her ideas became popular owing to Alexandra Kollontai – the main proponent of her views in Russia.[2] Following Zetkin, Kollontai depicted the woman question as a battlefield where two forces, the 'bourgeoisie' and the 'proletariat', ideologically confront and form two women's movements, the feminist and the socialist. Bolsheviks praised this rhetorical opposition which helped them to shape their politics. Zetkin's close relations with V I Lenin and Nadezhda Krupskaya also promoted her position as a respected communist who was 'inclined to make mistakes but was able to correct them'.[3] Her efforts devoted to the formation of the Communist Party of Germany (KPD) and her strong anti-fascist stand were appreciated in Soviet Russia as well. She took her last refuge in the Soviet Union where she died and was buried, interred in the wall of the Kremlin in 1933.

This chapter will explore the reception of Clara Zetkin in Russia in the period of the construction of the new state and new society. For the most part, I will address Zetkin's contacts in the Russian and soviet ruling circles and her role and place in the politics of the Soviet Union. In conclusion, I will dwell on how soviet propaganda exploited the name of Clara Zetkin to establish her in the pantheon of the heroes of the revolution. Today, the attitude to her work in Russia where she was respected first of all as a Marxist is closely linked to the approach to the 'woman question'. The complex and complicated ways of solving that 'question' in Soviet Russia have determined the place of Zetkin's heritage in Russian history.

Zetkin and Kollontai

It is well known that Clara Zetkin established close links with Russian socialist circles long before the 1900s. Soviet biographers point to the fact that soon after her family moved to Leipzig, young Clara Eissner made friends with a Russian student, Varvara, who introduced her to the émigré milieu.[4] There she met Ossip Zetkin, the Russian revolutionary in exile who was to become her partner and father of her two sons, Maxim and Konstantin. Towards the end of the century Clara Zetkin grew to be an outstanding figure in the Social Democratic Party of Germany (SPD) and the Second International, a politician with authority and charisma acknowledged worldwide and appreciated by Russian socialists and Marxists. The latter prized her as a theorist of the 'woman question' and the founder and chief strategist of the international socialist women's movement. Zetkin's publications together with August Bebel's book on women's emancipation, translated into Russian and extensively popularised in the early 1900s, inspired and recruited new generations of revolutionaries and were 'must read' texts for political radicals.[5] Kollontai, who played the key role in organising women workers under the banner of Marxism, confessed in her autobiography that Clara Zetkin 'exerted great influence upon her work on the formation of the grassroots proletarian women's movement in Russia'.[6] Kollontai emphasised the importance of the German experience as 'the cradle of the women's socialist movement'.[7] In her analytical *Zhenskoe rabochee dvizhenie* (1913), dealing with the women's labour movement, she wrote that 'Germany is the most characteristic state [...] while others [...] just replicate, with some insignificant variations, the path of the German socialist movement and adopt its main type'.[8]

Indeed, the concern around women workers' political activism was the main point of contact between Russian social democrats and Clara Zetkin before the October revolution of 1917. Angelica Balabanova became acquainted with her in Leipzig in the late 1890s; Krupskaya met Zetkin in 1902 in Bavaria; Lenin was introduced to her at the congress of the Second International in Stuttgart in 1907.[9] However, only Alexandra Kollontai developed a most intensive cooperation with Zetkin in this period. Kollontai, as a representative of the first socialist women workers' club in St Petersburg, was delegated to the International Socialist Women's Conference that preceded the congress of the Second International in 1907.[10] From this time on, she was recruited as a Russian correspondent of *Die Gleichheit*, writing as a public speaker on women's emancipation issues. Kollontai joined Zetkin as a guest speaker of the Adult Suffrage Society meeting in London in 1909.[11] At the next International Socialist Women's Conference in 1910, she was elected a member of the central bureau of the Socialist Women's International (SWI).[12]

Undoubtedly, Kollontai as a Marxist feminist theorist and activist developed under the guidance of Clara Zetkin. Of course, before she first met Zetkin in 1906, Kollontai had arrived at ideas about the need to unite women workers against 'bourgeois feminists'.[13] The latter became active at the outset of the first revolution in Russia in early 1905, gaining political influence and forming new associations in the interests of all women. Kollontai attended 'ladies' meetings', as she called them irritably, to provoke sharp discussions on class matters, but her first real steps towards mobilising women workers in Russia followed her visit to Zetkin in Germany. She initiated a club in St Petersburg – the Women Workers' Mutual Aid Society – and published articles advocating Marxist views on the woman question in the manner of Zetkin's rhetoric, and informing of the trends and developments in the international socialist women's movement.[14] Her voluminous book on the woman question, *Socialnyye osnovy zhenskogo voprosa* (1909), gives a comprehensive overview of the emergent Russian feminist movement between 1905 and 1908. Kollontai's devotion to German social democratic ideology and her self-representation as a Marxist determined her reasoning and conclusions, which centred around the confrontation of the two worlds, 'bourgeois' and 'proletarian', and, consequently, the two women's movements, feminist and socialist. The language of denunciation that the author used in her analysis of Russian feminists as well as her hasty generalisations were also conditioned by specific political attitudes held by Kollontai on the eve of the First All-Russian Women's Congress that took place in December 1908. She was ready to fight against her political opponents.[15]

Apart from her leading role in shaping women workers' organisations in Russia, Kollontai was instrumental as a member of the SWI. Following Zetkin's recommendations and at times her direct instructions, she made speeches and delivered lectures in Europe and the United States on a variety of topics such as the conditions of Russian women and IWD celebrations in Russia or social insurance and maternal allowances in European countries.

Zetkin's letters to Kollontai dated 1909 to 1914 abound in details of their complex collaboration, which intensified on the eve of the international socialist women's conferences.[16]

The outbreak of the First World War in 1914 made it problematic for Kollontai and Zetkin to work and communicate as before. Kollontai was in Germany when war was declared; she was arrested on 3 August 1914 by the German authorities but held only briefly. When released, she went to Denmark, then to Sweden where she was again arrested as an anti-war agitator. She was deported from Sweden in late November 1914 and after a short stay in Denmark, settled in Norway. Following Lenin's recommendations, Kollontai left for the USA for a propaganda and fundraising tour in early October 1915.[17] She made one more trip from Norway to the United States in 1916 and, in March 1917, returned to Russia to take an active part in Bolshevik politics.[18] Kollontai was not able to attend the 1915 International Socialist Women's Conference in Berne under the leadership of Zetkin but she did send greetings to Berne from Norway. Interestingly, another Russian socialist, Angelica Balabanova, who was active in the Italian Socialist Party, assisted Zetkin in the preparation of the conference.[19] The Russian delegation of six, including Inessa Armand and Nadezhda Krupskaya, served as Lenin's 'diplomatic envoys' trying to radicalise conference resolutions. While Zetkin preferred a simple denunciation of the war, the Russians criticised the belligerent nations' parties for approving war credits and called for revolutionary action.[20] Kollontai in her message to the Berne conference declared support for Lenin's line.[21] However, a moderate resolution was passed, evoking a reply on the part of the Russian delegates: 'We reject it on the grounds that it is incomplete and insufficient, but we do not rule out future cooperation'.[22]

Some historians emphasise tensions that were supposedly increasing between the two women, Zetkin and Kollontai, over the clash of opinions. For example, Beatrice Farnsworth claims that 'it was not likely that a friendship between strong-minded and combative people like Zetkin and Kollontai could evolve without friction' and points to some political disagreements and their rivalry in the International Women's Secretariat that was established by the Third International in 1920.[23] It appears most likely that Zetkin distanced herself from Kollontai after events known as the Workers' Opposition appeal in early 1922. As a leader of the Opposition, Kollontai was summoned before the Third International's Central Control

Commission; Zetkin, a member of the Commission, preferred to side with Lenin and his followers against the oppositionists, and Kollontai vanished from the proscenium of Bolshevik politics and from Zetkin's sight.[24]

Zetkin and the Russian Revolution

After the Bolshevik revolution in Russia, when the idea of the world socialist revolution became a driving force for the adherents of communism, Zetkin's cooperation with 'Russian friends' was built on projects of the Third International and inspired by expectations of 'the world revolutionary fire'.[25] Zetkin welcomed the Russian 'proletarian revolutions' of 1905 and 1917 and, in June 1918, sent a letter to Lenin expressing her support for the Russian soviet republic and assuring him that her 'heart and mind are with the Bolsheviks and the soviet government'.[26] Zetkin's open break with the SPD was a sign of her recognition of the leading role of the Bolsheviks in the international communist movement. In her eyes, Lenin grew into a cult figure.

The Russian revolution changed Zetkin's life greatly. After the First World War, she spent most of her time in Russia, taking part in affairs of the Third International while also remaining active in German politics and coping with serious illness. Zetkin explained her desire to come and stay in Russia by her willingness to witness and participate in the great social experiment, though it is obvious that her residing in Weimar Germany was ceasing to be comfortable.[27] Numerous documents kept in Moscow archives give an insight into Zetkin's life and contacts at this period.[28] It is clear that her experiences and impressions of Russia fall into two parts, with Lenin's death as a turning point. In the beginning, all things Zetkin witnessed in the soviet republic she presented with enthusiasm and great expectations; later, the tone and content of her correspondence changed to some extent.

There is a discrepancy in the sources regarding the date of Zetkin's first visit to Soviet Russia. Her arrival in the autumn of 1920 has been mentioned most often; however Elena Stasova indicates that Zetkin went to Moscow for the first time in the spring of that year to take part in 'an international women's conference'.[29] A letter Zetkin sent from Moscow in March 1920, which is now kept in a Moscow repository, confirms Stasova's account.[30] During the previous years, Clara Zetkin had said repeatedly that she would be happy to go to revolutionary Russia at the earliest opportunity 'to have a breath of the air of the first soviet republic in the world'.[3] When she finally reached Moscow, she was a woman of 63 in poor health requiring continuous medical care. Zetkin suffered from serious diseases including a cataract, frostbitten feet, asthma and an unknown form of malaria; therefore Lenin and other members of the soviet government made every effort to accommodate her with comfort, warmth and peace, and what is more, treated Clara Zetkin as a high ranking soviet official.

Soon after the Bolshevik revolution, the new bureaucracy emerged which enjoyed special privileges and had access to various resources. After the soviet government moved from Petrograd to Moscow in March 1918, the luxurious imperial hotels, National and Metropol, located in the Moscow city centre, were transformed into the executives' residences and governmental offices now called the First House of the Soviets and the Second House of the Soviets, respectively. These buildings, although partially damaged during the revolutionary upheaval, still had all facilities for decent existence and became home to many influential soviet functionaries up to the time the government moved to the Kremlin. For instance, Leon Trotsky, Felix Dzerzhinsky and Yakov Sverdlov lived in the National and Lenin and Krupskaya shared its room 107 for a short period, while Nikolai Bukharin was located in the Metropol. As Angelica Balabanova recalled, Zetkin, weak and 'inclined to hysterics', was brought initially to an ordinary hotel where there was no staff to take care of her. Lenin found these conditions unbearable for such a figure and helped to lodge Zetkin in a more appropriate place.[32] In the end, Zetkin got a suite in the Metropol that signified the status she had within the emerging state hierarchy. To make her residence in Russia more productive, she was provided with secretaries, private doctors and nurses and was granted a dacha in Malakhovka village near Moscow. As her physical condition became aggravated, Clara Zetkin received medical treatment in the state sanatoria in Kislovodsk and Zheleznovodsk in the Caucasus region, and in Arkhangelskoye – the Princess Yusupov family estate, one of the wealthiest domains in imperial Russia that had been nationalised in 1918 and converted into 'the best sanatorium in the country' for party officials and Red Army officers. Against a background of the harsh reality of life in the country recovering after the disastrous civil war, these sanatoria appeared to be welfare oases for the new elite. Therefore, it seems that Soviet Russia turned into the most secure place to live and work for Clara Zetkin in the interwar period.

In the face of all the physical troubles Zetkin had to over-come, this period is nonetheless recorded as a time of usual political and social activity. She was involved in the international communist women's movement and Third International affairs as well as in the painful processes of building the KPD, and was quite active in Russia as an outstanding political figure. Remarkably, she tried to take advantage of her political position in the soviet republic to help her compatriots. When mass discharges of those linked to the KPD started in Weimar Germany, Zetkin used her authority and valuable relationships to assist people in getting out of difficulties. A letter sent to Nadezhda Krupskaya in February 1932 relates Zetkin's efforts to bring a German school teacher to the Soviet Union and find a job for her there, since this woman had lost her position in Wiesbaden because of her membership of the KPD.[33] Zetkin's corre-spondence contains many examples of this kind of request ad-dressed to Bolshevik leaders, and their frequency suggests that such appeals were usually satisfied.

While in Russia, Zetkin made long journeys to remote parts of the Soviet Union and visited labour communes and factories and spoke at meetings and in the proletarian clubs. She enthusiastically met with workers, peasants and the intelligentsia and was deeply impressed with the ways the people overcame hunger and hardship and with their devotedness to the ideals of communism. In her memoirs, Angelica Balabanova claimed that Clara Zetkin was ad-dicted to tribunes and ovations and that this was the only reason why she went to large meetings. In Balabanova's words, 'With all their might, the Bolsheviks made use of this flaw in her personality. They flattered her, invited her for *tête-à-têtes* and let her think that she was influencing their politics. They laughed at her naivety, especially when she criticised them for the fatal mistakes they had made in relation to the German communists. Nevertheless [...] Clara could not stand up against their flattery'. As a result, Balabanova concludes, Zetkin became one of the Bolshevik leaders' 'marionettes', endlessly faithful to the Soviet Union.[34]

Such a way of representing Zetkin's relationships with her Russian comrades leads to a certain underestimation of her person-al motives and aspirations at the time. The 'Bolshevising' of Clara Zetkin appeared not only in her readiness to serve the Bolsheviks for 'demonstrative purposes', but in her strong and sincere belief in the newly formed Soviet Union as a practical model for reaching the goals of communism and in the soviet people as free citizens eager

to sacrifice their lives for a better future.[35] Zetkin often called he
journeys 'propaganda trips' and courageously made her way t
problem regions for 'agitation work'. She went to the Caucasus ir
1923 and 1924 and visited Tiflis and Vladikavkaz in October 1924
immediately after the suppression of the Menshevik uprising. In th
summer of 1925, when famine and cholera had spread in Centra
Russia, the Ukraine and other provinces, she travelled down th
Volga River aboard a ship named after her and communicated witl
common people.[36] Her travel experience resulted in a series o
articles and pamphlets distributed through the Third Internationa
network, and in an international campaign to aid the starving
workers and peasants of Russia.[37] But her activity also had ar
immediate effect on those soviet men and women who had the
chance to look at and listen to the 'legendary Clara Zetkin'.[38] It is
well known that agitation is one of the most powerful instruments
for mobilisation and in view of this, it is problematic to name
Zetkin's position in Russia as 'decorative' or 'demonstrative'. She
inspired people and made them think and act in accordance witl
the ideals of communism.

After Lenin's death

Zetkin's productive work in Soviet Russia was carried out against a
backdrop of gradual changes in the soviet ruling circles. She was
deeply shaken by Lenin's death in January 1924, and from that
time Zetkin regarded as her duty the task of bringing knowledge
about the leader of the Russian revolution to the world. In her
Reminiscences of Lenin, published in Russian in 1924, Zetkin
declared that she was obliged to share the 'treasury' of her personal
recollections of the 'unforgettable leader and friend' as it was her
'obligation' with respect to Vladimir Il'ich.[39] In Zetkin's words, 'this
is the obligation with respect to those to whom he had devoted all
his work: proletarians, the working people, the exploited and the
dependent from all over the world, all those embraced by his loving
heart and whom his proud mind regarded as revolutionary fighters
and makers of a more advanced social order'.[40] Zetkin valued Lenin
as a Marxist theorist and praised his personality, pointing to his
devotedness to the communist idea, his precise mind and his
modesty in private life. Although she was thirteen years older than
Lenin, in her writings Zetkin positioned herself as his follower and
admirer, ready to conform to his lines of argument. Her memoirs are
still a valuable source for studying the Russian leader, and they also

give a clue to understanding Clara Zetkin's character and views, especially in relation to her Russian political experience. It seems her enthusiasm for the soviet model of democracy coincided with her strong personal attachment to the Bolshevik leaders and this prevented Zetkin from thinking objectively about the reality of the situation in the Soviet Union. However, she was quite aware of changes in the Bolshevik Party's Central Committee, and her correspondence shows that she was well informed about the nuances of the struggle for leadership within the party.[41] In this confrontation, Zetkin found herself as one of the 'Old Bolsheviks' who felt the pressure the new regime was trying to impose.[42] It is unlikely that she communicated with Joseph Stalin and could envisage the course of events; what seriously depressed her at this time was the suspicion that her correspondence was inspected. In a letter to Elena Stasova in February 1924, Zetkin wrote about her intention to speak to Grigorii Zinoviev, then head of the Third International and one of the most influential soviet officials, on the matter. This feeling of being controlled did not leave her for years.[43]

Despite these events, Zetkin never showed any public display of disappointment. She continued to publish and speak in support of the Soviet Union, especially the way it liberated women from the chains of capitalism. Firmly believing in international solidarity among the working classes, Zetkin dedicated her efforts to the cause of worldwide communist revolution that would help to realise her dream of a new society free of oppression. Publishing articles and pamphlets about communist transformation in the Soviet Union, about its leaders and ordinary people, and about patterns of life in Russia was Zetkin's form of fighting for the spread of communism throughout the world. Up until her death, she was active as 'a soldier of the revolution'.[44]

In the late 1920s and early 1930s, the name and figure of Clara Zetkin had enormous popularity in Russia. During her journeys, she was open to new contacts and readily spent time among common people. She received dozens of letters from all parts of the Soviet Union with greetings on her birthday and for IWD celebrations, or expressing support for her opposition to the German government. Her Russian admirers paid tribute to her greatness, sending her various small presents, as practical as winter boots or food, or more symbolic as albums and souvenirs. The soviet leaders also displayed respect for her. She was awarded two of the highest honours of the Soviet Union: the Red Banner Order in 1927 and the

Lenin Order in 1933. Zetkin spent the last months of her life in Arkhangelskoye treated by the best doctors from the Kremlin hospital. She was buried in the heart of the soviet capital, on Red Square in the Kremlin wall – the highest honour a soviet citizen could receive. In soviet propaganda, Clara Zetkin became an icon in her lifetime. Her dedication to Marxism and Bolshevism as well as her loyalty to the leaders of the Russian October revolution had helped to create her image as 'the best friend of the Soviet Union' and 'Babushka kommunizma' ('the grandmother of communism').[45]

Zetkin's contribution to the Third International and her presidency of the International Red Aid (MOPR) from 1925 to 1927 stood as Zetkin's primary achievements that overshadowed her activity as the leader of the communist women's international. Starting in 1934, MOPR regularly published brochures and leaflets under the headline 'Clara Zetkin calls to international solidarity' and with similar content to refresh the memory of this 'Soldier of the Revolution' and, consequently, to attract more supporters to the idea of worldwide communist revolution. The day of Zetkin's death was declared the MOPR international recruiting day.[46]

In the obituaries written on Zetkin's death, Krupskaya developed another line of thinking about Zetkin as a highly respected Marxist theorist and educator. Again, the virtues Krupskaya prized in Zetkin were related to the struggle for proletarian revolution worldwide. What was important for Krupskaya was that Lenin had 'appreciated Clara for her fervent faith in the proletarian cause, for endless devotion to the cause of Revolution, for understanding of the tasks of the cultural revolution'.[47]

Today in Russia, there is no tradition to reflect and esteem Clara Zetkin as a leader of the women's movement. In the 1930s, the Russian proponents of women's issues had already been removed from the political scene and this side of Zetkin's activity was doomed to oblivion. Even with the revival of feminism in Russia in the 1990s, Zetkin's legacy was not recalled and her name appeared only in relation to writings devoted to Kollontai. The pantheon of the heroes of the Russian revolution had been destroyed. The history of the women's movements in Russia is still taking its first steps. The figure of Clara Zetkin, a woman truly loved in that country, should be restored in the history and collective memory of Russians.

Chapter Four

Defamed in the West, Idealised in the East? On the Reception of Clara Zetkin in Germany after 1945[1]

Florence Hervé

For the Emperor Wilhelm II, she was 'the most dangerous witch' of the German Empire; for the social democrats Lily Braun and Marie Juchacz, a dominating person who rejected everybody who disagreed with her. But Minna Cauer, a radical feminist of the bourgeois movement, was full of admiration: 'What a woman! If we just had such women among us'. The feminist and pacifist Helene Stöcker was impressed by the courage of Clara Zetkin, 'by her passion in acting, by the absolute integrity of her character and by her warm humanity'.[2] Today there are still divergent opinions about Clara Zetkin: was she an antifeminist and dogmatic communist, a bourgeois or a socialist fighter for women's rights? There are in Germany few personalities of the women's movement who are looked at so differently.

In the political landscape, Clara Zetkin is known as a representative of the proletarian women's movement, as a socialist, communist and anti-militarist. But few realise that she was a talented pedagogue, too, an historian of art and literature, a brilliant speaker and a rebel in both her private and political lives. Trade unions and women's groups celebrate International Women's Day (IWD) today, but few realise that Clara Zetkin was one of its major initiators.

Silence and detraction in the pre-unification Federal Republic of Germany (FRG)

During the Cold War, from the 1950s until the beginning of the 1960s, Clara Zetkin was 'persona non grata' and IWD was considered an event of the devil. Only the Communist Party of Germany (KPD), which was banned in 1952, and a few women's groups such as the Demokratischer Frauenbund Deutschlands (Democratic women's league of Germany, outlawed in 1957) and the Westdeutsche Frauenfriedensbewegung (Movement of West German women for peace) commemorated 8 March and evoked its initiator.

45

At the end of the sixties, with the easing of the political situation and the rise of new social movements, feminists rediscovered Clara Zetkin. One part of the feminist movement considered Zetkin responsible for the scission of the women's movement at the end of the nineteenth and beginning of the twentieth centuries. The journalist Alice Schwarzer writes in her bestseller *Der kleine Unterschied und seine großen Folgen* (1975), 'The illegitimate separation of the women's movement into bourgeois and proletarian means the negation of specific discriminations of women and reduces the women's question to a class problem'.[3] Another journalist, Marielouise Janssen-Jurreit, argues in a similar way in another bestseller, *Sexismus. Über die Abtreibung der Frauenfrage* (1976): 'Clara Zetkin refused the struggle of the sexes and fought after 1889 against feminism and feminists'.[4] However, in those writings, the critics did not take account of the context of the early women's movement – the different social situations, problems and conflicts – nor of the evolution of Clara Zetkin's position towards the organisation of women.

In the first socialist-feminist groups such as Aktionsrat zur Befreiung der Frau (Action council for the liberation of women) in West Berlin and Arbeitskreis Emanzipation (Working group for emancipation) in Bonn at the end of the 1960s, female students discussed Marxist writings (August Bebel, Friedrich Engels, Zetkin) as well as Simone de Beauvoir, and took over the tradition of 8 March. They appreciated the actuality of Zetkin's thoughts about women's labour at a time when the government's and media's ideal for women was that of housewives. Zetkin's writings provided arguments for the necessity of women's work and for the value of labour for the emancipation of women.

At that time, there were very few publications available by or about Clara Zetkin. Two of them were published by far left publishers: a reprint of Zetkin's *Zur Geschichte der proletarischen Frauenbewegung in Deutschland* (1979) by Verlag Marxistische Blätter and Karin Bauer's biography, *Clara Zetkin und die proletarische Frauenbewegung* (1978), published by Oberbaum Verlag, which insists on the necessity of class struggle for women's emancipation.[5]

Marxist circles referred themselves mainly to publications of the East German Pädagogische Hochschule Clara Zetkin (Clara Zetkin pedagogical college) in Leipzig. The Verlag Marxistische Blätter published Zetkin's *Zur Geschichte der proletarischen Frauenbewegung Deutschlands* (1978) and *Für die Sowjetmacht* (1977) as vell as articles and speeches concerning the October revolution, Lenin and the situation in the Soviet Union. In her 1981 portrait of Clara Zetkin, the well-known writer Gisela Elsner refutes the criticism that Zetkin was responsible for the scission of the women's movement, emphasising that Zetkin recognised some progressive ideas of the bourgeois movement on women's work and the vote.[6]

In the 1980s, the German Communist Party (DKP) organised two conferences, on the 50th anniversary of Zetkin's death Stuttgart, 1983) and for her 130th birthday (Wuppertal, 1987). A brochure with Zetkin's texts on women's labour was published, in which paid employment is presented as central to women's emancipation.[7]

The Social Democratic Party of Germany (SPD) practically ignored Clara Zetkin, while the mood in the German Federation of Trade Unions (DGB) was to disregard IWD. In 1980, 'for the sake of trade union unity', the DGB decided not to participate in the 8 March demonstrations since the day is 'inspired by the resolution of the second International Women's Congress in Copenhagen 1910' and is a 'political party day'.[8] The instructions of the DGB leadership were not followed. Gisela Kessler, at that time the women's secretary and vice-president of the media trade union, described the revolt: 'There came more and more resolutions in favour of 8 March, and the DGB itself was obliged to call for demonstrations'.[9] Since that time, the trade unions have commemorated the date.

In the 1980s, university research on Zetkin was still rare, but more differentiated than during the early Cold War and it concentrated on Zetkin's SPD period (1889-1917). In her book *Die geteilte Utopie. Sozialisten in Frankreich und in Deutschland* (1985), Marieluise Christadler compares Clara Zetkin with personalities of the French feminist movement like Louise Michel, Louise Saumoneau and Hubertine Auclert. In the same collection, Friedhelm Boll also compares Clara Zetkin with Hubertine Auclert:

> Both women had a strong radicalism, which expressed itself in different ways depending upon the political context of their two countries: spectacular actions and appeals on the one hand, a continuity of organisational work on the other. Differences existed about the form of the struggle but not about the importance of publicity. [...] Another similarity was the relation of equality of both women with their partners.[10]

The only FRG book devoted entirely to Clara Zetkin was by the American researcher Joan Reutershan, *Clara Zetkin und Brot und*

Rosen (1985), which focuses on the political conflicts between party and women's movement in the SPD before the First World War. The book highlights Clara Zetkin's positions on the role of culture and literature in class struggle and the necessity of socialist literature in the socialist movement.[11]

Glorification and Research in the German Democratic Republic (GDR)

In the GDR, Zetkin was revered as a heroine, embodying the struggle for revolution, socialism and women's rights. She was put on a pedestal. Medals and stamps carried her image; many roads and places, factories and schools were named after her; and IWD was celebrated everywhere on 8 March. Zetkin was idealised as the model woman who succeeded in combining work, family and politics. She was described by Luise Dornemann as the 'true friend of the Soviet Union', 'a loving woman and caring mother', a 'fighter against imperialism and fascism, for peace and socialism, a proletarian internationalist, a fighter for women's freedom'.[12]

Nevertheless, some aspects of Clara Zetkin's life were not revealed, such as her opposition to Joseph Stalin and the Third International, her disagreements with the KPD in the Weimar Republic and her life with her SPD husband, Friedrich Zundel. In one of the first Zetkin biographies, which reached nine editions between 1957 and 1989, Dornemann dedicated only 50 out of 550 pages to the last ten years of Zetkin's life. Zetkin's criticism of communist politics is not revealed.[13] In 1964, a book for young teenagers entitled *Das Mädchen aus Wiederau* by Lilo Hardel was published describing the young rebellious Clara. The story ends with Zetkin's choice of class struggle and love for the Russian revolutionary Ossip Zetkin.[14]

From 1955, collections of Zetkin's texts and extracts from her books began publication in the GDR, among them her history of the proletarian women's movement and her views on fascism, and Lenin.[15] Memorials were inaugurated in 1956, in Clara Zetkin's birthplace of Wiederau, Saxony, and in 1957 in Birkenwerder near Berlin, her last German residence.[16] The principal centre of research on Clara Zetkin was the Institut für Marxismus-Leninismus (Institute for Marxism-Leninism) in Berlin. It published, among others things, Clara Zetkin's *Zur Theorie und Taktik der kommunistischen Bewegung*, under the editorship of Katja Haferkorn and Heinz Karl (1974).[17]

Four other institutions dedicated themselves to research on Zetkin. The Humboldt University, Berlin, focussed from the middle of the 1950s on Zetkin as a pedagogue. Zetkin had received an education as a teacher and had taken a position on pedagogical and school politics in several speeches. In the GDR, Zetkin was considered a classical theoretician of socialist pedagogy, who fought for a unique secular school system. Several books were published, among them Zetkin's texts on youth education, on proletarian family education, on revolutionary school politics and Zetkin's speeches and writings on education, politics and Marxist pedagogy.[18] The Akademie für Gesellschaftswissenschaften beim Zenralkomitee der SED (Academy for the social sciences at the central committee of the Socialist Unity Party) promoted Zetkin as a representative of Marxist aesthetics. Emilia Milowidowa, Zetkin's daughter-in-law, reprinted her articles on literature and art which had originally been published in *Die Gleichheit*, while a volume of Zetkin's articles and thoughts about art and literature was also published in 1977 under the title *Kunst und Proletariat*.[19] From the 1980s, the Ernst-Moritz-Arndt-University in Greifswald published research on Zetkin as a theoretician on economic and state questions.[20]

In 1966 in Leipzig, a group of researchers founded a unique research centre – the Sektion Geschichte der Pädagogischen Hochschule Clara Zetkin, Forschungsgemeinschaft 'Geschichte des Kampfes der Arbeiterklasse für die Befreiung der Frau' (History section of the Clara Zetkin pedagogical college's research group, History of the working class struggle for the liberation of women'). It organised academic conferences from 1968 until 1989, while theses on Clara Zetkin and chronicles on the women's movement were published. It had international contacts, not only with Eastern Bloc countries, but to personalities in France, Great Britain, the USA and the FRG. In December 1991, after the dissolution of the Pädagogische Hochschule at the end of the GDR, it was replaced by the association, 'Frauen in der Geschichte' (Women in history), but that only lasted for a few years.[21]

In comparison to the FRG, the reception of Clara Zetkin was more differentiated in the GDR. On the one hand, there is a certain hagiography and an inexact representation of her relations to the KPD at the end of the Weimar Republic, while on the other, a detailed knowledge of her life and work, mainly from her SPD period 1889-1917).

Since German reunification

After the fall of the Berlin Wall, Clara Zetkin seems to have been 'forgotten' in German history. In 1991 to mark the occasion of the centenary of *Die Gleichheit* (1891-1923), the archives of the Archiv der deutschen Frauenbewegung (Archive of the German women's movement, ADF) in Kassel published documentation of the journal which was edited by Zetkin from 1892 to 1917.

But it was in France in 1993 and not in Germany that a new Zetkin biography was published. One problem in researching Zetkin's activities during the Cold War was that academics and researchers did not have full access to the Zetkin archives in Berlin and Moscow; many documents and letters were marked as 'confidential', *gesperrt* or *vertraulich*. With the end of the Cold War the French historian and Germanist Gilbert Badia was able to consult the Zetkin papers. His book was translated and published in Germany in 1994 by Dietz in Berlin. Many publishing houses in western Germany had refused it 'because Clara Zetkin does not interest anybody today'.[22] Badia describes a new Clara Zetkin rebellious, opposed to Stalin and to the orientations of the Third International and also to the KPD.

A comparison of the reception of Badia's book in France and in Germany shows major differences that reflect ideological impacts and tendencies in Germany. Within one year, 2,000 copies of the book on the German political leader were sold in France – in Germany it took six years to reach that figure! In France there were many, mainly positive reviews of Badia's book. In Germany the few reviews published were mostly negative.[23] The social democratic newspaper *Vorwärts* - Forward - planned a précis of it that was never published. The well-known liberal weekly *Die Zeit* - The times - wrote: 'Clara Zetkin was in the shadow of her comrade Rosa Luxemburg. [...] She had no humour and no spirit. [...] Clara was already in her appearance strict and oldish. A museum figure which hardly interests anybody in 1994'.[24] Tânia Puschnerat, who wrote her thesis on Clara Zetkin, considered Badia's biography 'very problematic [...] because it is imbued with apologetic intentions making Zetkin a hero. [...] One misses a critical and objective perspective'.[25] Only the historians Marielouise Christadler and Friedhelm Boll emphasised Badia's scientific and at the same time popular approach, the 'differentiated portrait of the politician', and onsidered the book very well written and had 'a lot of fun reading '.[26]

The year 1994, when Badia's biography was being debated, ʻas also the year in which the government of Berlin decided that ʻlara Zetkin's name was unworthy for the road leading to the ʻarliament building, as she was a 'supporter of a communist ictatorship' and partly responsible for the 'destruction of the first ʻerman democracy, the Weimar Republic'. Zetkin's name was ʻeplaced by that of Princess Dorothea von Brandenburg. The office f Chancellor Helmut Kohl intervened personally against the name f Zetkin. The change occurred in spite of many protests from the ʻniversities of Connecticut, Illinois, Louisville and Paris, from the ʻolitical parties SPD, the Party of Democratic Socialism (PDS) and ʻhe Green Party in Berlin, from the Aktives Museum (Activist muse-ʻm) of fascism and resistance in Berlin, from the Bundes-Arbeitsge-ʻeinschaft kommunaler Frauenbüros (Federal working group of ʻommunal women's desks), the Landesarbeitsgemeinschaft der ʻezirklichen Frauen- und Gleichstellungsbeauftragten (Regional ʻorking group of cantonal equal opportunity commissioners), the ʻandeskonferenz der Frauenbeauftragten an Hochschulen (Region-ʻl conference of equal opportunity commissioners at universities) in ʻerlin, from university women's groups like the Zentrum für inter-ʻisziplinäre Frauenforschung (Centre for interdisciplinary women's ʻtudies) and the Frauenbeauftragte (Women's bureau) of Humboldt ʻniversity in Berlin, and from feminist groups such as the Arbeits-ʻemeinschaft sozialdemokratischer Frauen (Working group of so-ʻial-democratic women) in Berlin, Arbeitskreis wissenschaftlich und ʻünstlerisch tätiger Frauen (Working group of women artists and ʻesearchers) in Berlin, the ADF in Kassel and the Europäische ʻrauen Aktion (European women's action) in Berlin.[27] In eastern ʻermany many roads lost 'Clara Zetkin' from their names. Zetkin is ʻo longer evoked in schoolbooks. The well-known writer Christa ʻolf comments that behind these decisions there is the will 'to erase ʻft identity in the towns and in the thoughts of people'.[28] Badia ʻeclared, 'As an historian, I am very worried about the plans for the ʻradication of such a personality'.[29]

In 1995, almost one hundred years after its first publication, ʻer Student und das Weib (Student and woman) (1899), a speech by ʻetkin which had not appeared in her selected works in the GDR, ʻas finally reprinted in a German journal (it had previously ap-ʻeared in France in 1980).[30] It is interesting to observe that this

51

speech, which is most important for Zetkin's feminism and her views on the relations between men and women, marriage and divorce, is hardly cited by German Zetkin researchers today. In 2003, a controversial new biography of Zetkin appeared by Tânia Puschnerat, in which the author emphasises Zetkin's 'bourgeois mentality'.[31] Two other portraits of Zetkin were published in 2005 by Gisela Greulich-Janssen and Irma Hildebrandin, in books which are devoted to women's struggles for socialism and to courageous women of the last five centuries, respectively.[32]

Since the middle of the first decade of the twenty-first century, a modest revival in interest in Zetkin has occurred. In May 2006, the left party, Die Linke (a merger of the PDS and other left groups), inaugurated its office 'Clara Zetkin' in the German Bundestag. Then, on the occasion of the 150th anniversary of Clara Zetkin's birth in 2007, debate re-emerged around Zetkin's relevance. Several publications showed a new interest in this feminist personality of the working class movement. Thus, *Clara Zetkin oder Dort kämpfen, wo das Leben ist* was published, which includes a biographical essay and unpublished or out-of-print texts by Zetkin. Conferences took place at the University of Leipzig ('Die Frauenpolitikerin Clara Zetkin' [The women's political leader Clara Zetkin]) and in Berlin and Stuttgart, commemorating 100 years of the International Socialist Congress in Stuttgart. These resulted in a few articles being published, some television and radio broadcasts, and lectures in several cities.[33] Also in 2007, IG-Metall-Frauen (women of the metallurgical trade union) of Heidenheim initiated a Clara Zetkin Prize to reward commitment to the women's cause.

In 2009 the association, Waldheim-Stuttgart e.V. Clara Zetkin-Haus in Sillenbuch, celebrated its centenary with a number of activities, among them the publication of a brochure with a short biography and an article on Zetkin's relevance. This commune of the socialist workers' movement for the recreation and education of working class families was founded by Zetkin and others in 1909 and took her name in 1972.[34]

In relation to the centenary of the creation of IWD in 2010 the well-known feminist journalist Alice Schwarzer evoked Clara Zetkin as a 'definitively anti-feminist socialist' and called for the abolition of the celebration as a socialist and East German invention and a substitute for Mother's Day.[35] But some interest in Zetkin was generated by the occasion and in 2010 a reprint of Clara Zetkin's

907 speech on women's suffrage, *Zur Frage des Frauenwahlrechts*, as published in Bremen.[36]

In two reference books containing documents on feminist theory and the feminist movement published in 2010, Clara Zetkin is still depicted as responsible for the scission of the women's movement.[37] On the internet platform 'Fembio', featuring biographies of women, Susanne Gretter's portrait of Zetkin is illustrated with past GDR stamps, medals, banknotes and coins, emphasising the East German communist character of Zetkin.[38] In most publications, her international character is hardly mentioned and then only in relation to IWD.

The controversial debate about Clara Zetkin is not yet over. Zetkin has still to be (re)discovered in Germany, away from hagiography and detraction and beyond political disputes. It is to be hoped that Zetkin's complete works will eventually be published.

Clara Zetkin and Rosa Luxemburg in 1910

Chapter Five

Clara Zetkin Goes International: The Socialist Women's International and Unequal European and Global Order, 1907 to 1917

Susan Zimmermann

This chapter explores two dimensions of the history of the Socialis Women's International (SWI) between 1907 and the years of th First World War, namely representational politics within the SWI and its self-positioning and politics in relation to peace and wai While showing how Clara Zetkin sought to use the SWI to create ai international bridge across territorial boundaries, I argue that thes two fields of action were at the core of how the SWI positioned itse. in relation to inequality in international and domestic orders. To large extent the politics of the SWI in these and other spheres c activity were shaped by Zetkin, as international secretary of th organisation, and by the political worldview of the specific group c socialists to which she belonged. In addition, the SWI's politics ca1 be understood in an adequate manner only if read against develop ments that characterised both male-dominated socialist interna tionalism, that is, the Second International established in 1889, an the International Woman Suffrage Alliance (IWSA) founded in 1904 a close non-socialist neighbour of the SWI.

I will first situate my study of these two fields of action of th SWI within a broader set of questions about the relationship be tween internationalist activism and global inequality. I will the1 discuss how representational politics pursued within the SWI wer characterised by a specific ambiguity, especially when it came to th representation of nations without a state. The next section discuss es the critique of 'imperialist war', a cornerstone of both the engage ment of the SWI with transnational and domestic inequality and it overall political self-positioning. In conclusion I argue that the SW pursued its politics in these two spheres of activity with a view t explicitly positioning itself in relation to political dynamics an inequalities within countries, on the international plane, and amon neighbouring internationalist organisations.

International movements and global inequality

My study of the relationship between the SWI's internationalist politics and activism on the one hand and inequality in the international and domestic order on the other is informed by a more general argument on the often overlooked centrality of the engagement of international activism with the global inequality that was a deeply ingrained feature of the international system.[1] Like all international organisations aiming to improve the fate of majority populations or of particularly exploited groups both nationally and internationally, the politics of the SWI in the early twentieth century could not avoid relating to transnational material inequality and unequal power relations within the international order. The response of these international organisations to global inequality can be traced on three core levels.

First, in their internal politics international organisations had to take a stand regarding the unequal status of various groups and territories within the international order. In their representational politics, for example, they had to decide in which way affiliated organisations, such as 'sections' in the case of the Second International, would or would not stand in for the empires, states, nations without a state or other dominated territories and groups that they were to represent internationally, or how these affiliated sections were to represent social organisations or movements in other ways. Political decision-making in this area formed one element of the history of how within their own house international movements replicated or challenged the dominance within Europe and beyond of empires in the international system within and against which they had to operate. The internal institutional strategies and policies pursued by organised international movements in this way can be understood as a faithful portrait of how they positioned themselves vis-à-vis western dominance, and vis-à-vis political claims informed by the struggle for national self-determination and against imperial and colonial domination. At the same time the international movements themselves often conceived of their internal politics as a purely pragmatic, organisational matter. Yet sometimes, and especially once certain groups challenged what they perceived as structures of domination engrained in rules, regulations and practices inside international organisations, the relationship between internationalist internal politics on the one hand and pre-existing structures of global inequality on the other was discussed in overtly political terms.

A second layer of the political response of international movements to transnational inequality was their political self-positioning and intervention in questions explicitly or implicitly related to power and inequality in the international arena. Internationalists positioned themselves in relation to, and intervened or did not intervene in, problems of colonialism and imperialism, war and anti-war politics, the international (re-)distribution of resources, racism, international relations, and so forth. For some international organisations these issues formed part of their actual agenda, while for others they fell outside the scope of their self-defined mission. It is important to note that a politics of not addressing these phenomena amounted to an implicit statement about patterns of global inequality. Such silence could indicate acceptance of, or – if for tactical reasons only – tolerance towards, the related phenomena. An international women's organisation for example could pursue a politics of silence as to the question of national self-determination either because it opposed the politics of national self-determination that challenged pre-existing empires or because it wished to foreground the woman question narrowly defined in order to unite as many women as possible for this one goal. In reality, however, such politics might actually alienate women not willing to prioritise the woman question over self-determination.[2]

A third layer of how international movements addressed global inequality can be characterised as the patterns of interaction they created, promoted or avoided between their core agenda on the one hand and dynamics of global inequality and unequal international development on the other. How important were these issues to their mission? For example, if an international organisation focused on the extension of suffrage it could not but develop a certain strategy of dealing with the fact that the electoral systems in different countries, or portions of empires, were characterised by different forms and degrees of exclusion and inclusion. Elsewhere I have shown how the SWI internationalised the question of extending the vote to women in countries that still lacked universal male suffrage.[3] It is clear that in its representational and its anti-war politics, the SWI explicitly combined a focus on change in the international and domestic order.

Representing social revolution and the non-self-governing nation

From the outset, the SWI found itself in a rather peculiar position when it came to representational politics. This was due firstly to its close relationship with the Second International. On the one hand this relationship allowed for a substantial amount of political flexibility for the SWI in developing its representational politics as it could rely in principle on a pre-existing organisational structure. For this reason, there was no need for the new women's organisation to develop a highly formalised format in this field of politics, which in turn enabled it to pursue its representational politics without making explicit and potentially controversial statements about it.

Yet on the other hand the close relationship of the SWI with the Second International meant that the structures determining representation were in a sense pre-established. Secondly, the constellation of interests within the SWI with regard to representational politics also bore its specific traits. International representational politics formed one sphere of activity into which Clara Zetkin, the towering head of the organisation, had not been substantially involved earlier and her interest in this question appeared to be limited. At the same time, her close collaborator Rosa Luxemburg, who had begun her political career in a Polish socialist movement that was divided on this issue, had played an important role within the Second International's rather heated political struggles unfolding in the years before 1907 on the reform of representational politics. Luxemburg had an emphatic interest in the larger tension informing these reform endeavours, namely the relationship between socialism and nation or more precisely the issue of how international socialism was to position itself in relation to demands for national self-determination, especially but not exclusively in central and eastern Europe.

In the debates on organisational reform within the International Socialist Bureau (ISB), the core co-ordinating body of the Second International, Luxemburg had forcefully opposed organisational advances of the nation or nationality principle within international socialism. Already since the 1890s she had repudiated in principle and in relation to the Polish question in particular the phenomenon labelled 'social patriotism'. For Luxemburg the future of the Kingdom of Poland was territorial autonomy within a democratic Russian Republic rather than sovereign nationhood. This was so because of the ongoing economic integration of the industrialising kingdom into the larger empire.[4] This position on the question of independent representation within international socialism of nations without a state was grounded in a strong emphasis on class. It markedly differed from those tendencies in socialist and progressive non-socialist international movements inclined to be supportive (with whatever qualifications) of demands for self-government, and from the more conservative international organisations within the non-socialist camp that tended to shrink back from considering visible representation of non-self-governing nations.[5]

Taken together these factors resulted in specific ambiguity within the SWI as to the representation of nations without a state. In so far as the new women's organisation at its inaugural meeting on the eve of the Stuttgart congress of the Second International in 1907 wished to model its representational modalities on the precedent of the Second International, it could build on the new organisational statute that, as a result of the reform efforts of the preceding years, would be laid before and accepted by the Stuttgart congress. With this statute in the final stages of decision making and the women's organisation just being established, the SWI at its inaugural meeting enjoyed a considerable degree of freedom regarding the question of how to handle representation. The new organisational regulations of the Second International reformed principles of how its constituent units were built; that is, how the 'sections' were constructed and how they related to each other.

According to the new regulation the socialist parties and unions of 'each country [de chaque pays ou nation]' had to form a section which in turn had to decide about the affiliation of all organisations of the 'nationalities concerned [des pays ou nations concernés]'. In addition, the Second International for the first time in its history diversified the size and thus the political weight of the sections. From 1907 onwards they were to be composed of two to twenty members according to the criteria of the number of party/trade union members in relation to population of the given country, the 'importance of the nationality [de la nationalité]' in question and the political strength of the socialist organisations in the country.[6] The ambiguity in the language of the statute when referring to 'countries' and 'nationalities' was a faithful mirror of both the history of and the ongoing conflicts over the international representational politics within the Second International. Originally the International had been quite open to allotting full and equal representation to European nations without a state, especially as they fought for their freedom from political oppression within retrograde empires. The long-established Polish section was a case in point.

Yet the more organisations from nations without a state who conceived of themselves as (not only class-political but also) territorial entities sought separate representation within the international socialist movement, the more did the leftwing forces as represented on the top echelons of the International – among them Rosa Luxemburg – resist. The new organisational statute of 1907 was a compromise. It avoided any explicit or straightforward self-positioning of the International regarding its future representational politics vis-à-vis the complex problem of nation or state as points of reference. The statute combined acceptance of the inherited status quo, flexibility in handling future applications for separate affiliation by nations without a state, and an intention to control as well as hold back tendencies of further 'nationalisation' of the system of representation, i.e. the tendency to create new sections representing nations without a state or other minorities within the International. Accordingly, independent affiliation was to be considered only in cases where strong socialist organisations had developed that explicitly and exclusively related to nations without a state. Nevertheless, in the years after the Stuttgart congress the representational politics of the Second International based in the new statute and connected stipulations, which laid the final decision-making power about the admission of new sections in the hands of the ISB, would prove only partially successful in this regard. The number of separate sections constituted by socialist organisations representing nations without a state grew steadily. On top of this, a tendency of separate representation of 'nationalities' or minorities within pre-existing sections would gain momentum.[7]

Taken together, the Second International in its representational politics never subscribed to the territoriality principle to the extent other reform-minded or progressive international organisations of the time did. In defining the points of reference for its representational strategies, it referred to social movements on the ground rather than to pre-existing legal and political entities and regulations.

The SWI under Zetkin's leadership took for granted the same principle of an openly political rather than legalistic approach to representational politics. Yet within this framework it developed its own profile which in part differed from the developments in the Second International and in the IWSA. Already before the 1907 Stuttgart congress of the Second International a lead article in the biweekly *Die Gleichheit*, the (future) voice of the SWI, which was edited by Zetkin, sharply polemicised against any privilege of the national over the class principle. In the struggle with the propertied classes the 'proletarian masses' had to 'energetically stand for their class interest' instead of 'defending under all circumstances the bourgeois nation-state – the fatherland of the propertied'.[8] At the first International Conference of Socialist Women assembling on the eve of the Stuttgart congress, the leadership of the SWI on many levels followed the representational principles and practice to be pursued at the Stuttgart congress of the Second International which was based on the new organisational principles to be adopted at that congress.

Accordingly, the delegates or delegations accepted by the SWI were grouped so as to independently enlist Finland, Hungary and Norway, and the Cisleithanian delegation was listed under the heading 'Austria 9 (including 2 Czechs)'. Cisleithania was the part of the Habsburg Monarchy that colloquially was referred to as Austria but included large territories dominated or co-populated by Slavic minorities as opposed to the German Austrians. At the same time, the emerging SWI did not grant separate formal representation for any part of partitioned Poland.[9] This was in sharp contrast to the representational politics of the Second International, where a separate Polish section consisting of delegates from the Russian, Austrian and German lands of partitioned Poland as well as exile organisations were represented by a separate and independent section as early as the 1890s. The new organisational statute adopted in 1907 maintained the practice with reference to a politics of keeping pre-existing votes 'for the sake of peace and quiet'.[10]

Against this background the avoidance of any visible representation of Poland at the first conference of the SWI was most likely based on conscious and politically motivated decision-making. Women from Polish Russia who were present at the conference were presented accordingly. The conference report (not the official conference minutes) published in *Die Gleichheit* mentions '3 guests' who were present at the conference 'on behalf of organisations in Russia'. One of them was Comrade Wilkominski, the representative of '200 Jewish female weavers' from the industrial city of ŁódŸ in the Kingdom of Poland, the portion of partitioned Poland that belonged o the Russian Empire. In the official register of speakers the representative of the weavers from Łódŷ figured as 'Wilkominski Russia)', in the minutes of the speeches as 'Mrs Wilkominski-Lodz'. Other evidence similarly points to conscious avoidance of any representation of (whichever part of) Poland. While the conference regretted the absence of delegates from a number of countries, Poland, which did not represent an independent nation, was missing from the list. The only other group of European countries that would be represented at the Stuttgart congress of the Second International but was missing from the women's conference – and whose absence similarly was not noted – were the Balkan states of Rumania and Serbia and the not fully sovereign Bulgaria.[11]

Last but not least, Rosa Luxemburg could have easily made herself a representative of the Socjaldemokracja Królestwa Polskego i Litwy (Social Democracy of the Kingdom of Poland and of Lithuania, SDKPiL) at the women's conference. Within the Second International Luxemburg oftentimes represented this party, which stood for the anti-nationalist wing of the Polish labour movement and formed an important element of the Polish section.[12] Yet at the women's conference Luxemburg did not figure as a representative of this party, and the Polska Partia Socjalistyczna (Polish Socialist Party, PPS), which demanded 'independence and self-government for Poland' and was similarly active in the Second International, was absent as well.[13] Given her political position regarding the question of Polish independence, it may well have been the case that Luxemburg aimed at avoiding independent Polish representation. As long as there was no separate Polish delegation at all – as was the case at the 1907 conference of the SWI – it must have made sense to Luxemburg for her not to figure in the colours of the SDKPiL.

The obvious facts and tendencies regarding the management of the Polish question and the representation of other not fully sovereign or non-self-governing nations notwithstanding, the overall character of the ensemble of representational politics pursued by leadership of the SWI in Stuttgart in 1907 was nowhere spelled out; whatever strategy was pursued in this regard was kept implicit. The situation was similar in relation to the second conference of the SWI convened – as the last international peace time conference of socialist women – in Copenhagen in 1910. At the same time on this occasion particular circumstances forced Clara Zetkin and Rosa Luxemburg to take a more explicit position regarding the Polish question as compared to 1907. Prior to the Copenhagen conference

two emerging women's organisations belonging to the PPS which
were active in Cisleithania had sent in reports to be submitted to the
conference. One of these groups was the 'Polish social-democratic
women's organisation in Austrian-Silesia' (1907), the other one the
'Cracow women's organisation of the Polish social-democratic party
of Galicia and Silesia (Austrian-Poland)' (1909).[14] Most likely the
receipt of the Cracow report triggered the decision to plan for a
Polish delegation to the Copenhagen conference. Zetkin and Luxemburg now wished to take a proactive stance to secure a strong
anti-nationalist presence in the expected Polish delegation. Pointing
to the Cracow report Luxemburg wrote to Leo Jogiches, who at the
time belonged to the leadership of the SDKPiL:

> Zetkin has sent the attached nonsense from Galicia, and she
> considers it *indispensible* that from our side as well some two
> trulls [Weiber] shall travel and participate in the trulls' confer-
> ence (which will be held before the congress). [...] I consider as
> *absolutely indispensible* a delegation consisting of six individ-
> uals: Two women (besides me) and approximately two to three
> 'gentlemen'. In any case I need to be given a mandate for the
> trulls' conference, too.[15]

At the 1910 women's conference there was a Polish delegation
indeed, though from the documents to hand it is unclear to which
of the two parties, the SDKPiL or the PPS, the members belonged.
Among the speakers was comrade Perlmutter from L'viv/Lemberg/
Lwów, and the conference adopted resolutions submitted by the
Polish-Galician/Silesian comrades.[16] From then on the Polish
women's movement in Galicia was self-evidently treated as a com-
ponent of the SWI.[17]

In parallel the SWI at its 1910 conference took an explicit
political stance on the matter of national self-determination for the
first time. Zetkin and Luxemburg's leftwing socialist position clearly
determined the position of the SWI. A resolution passed at the
conference declared that the political freedom of Finland – which
country since 1906 enjoyed (again) autonomy within the Russian
Empire – was to be defended. This was so in the first place because
'the most democratic franchise of the world stands and falls' with
Finland's political freedom. Finland had introduced universal suffrage in 1906 and the working population of the country had won
the franchise in a dual struggle against the outer enemy, Tsarism,
and the inner enemy, the proprietary classes, through the
'revolutionary mass-strike'. Therefore 'suppression of the national

freedom of this country would result in especially strong political gagging of the working masses'. The Finnish Labour Party was a leading force in a struggle which was 'an episode in the history of the Russian Revolution out of whose victorious hands all peoples living under the Tsarist thumb will one day receive their national right of self-determination'.[18]

The resolution in this way named a whole number of historically concrete circumstances and conditions that lent a progressive character to the Finnish freedom struggle: Finnish democracy, the 'especially strong' suppression of the working classes which was to be anticipated if the Finnish case was lost, and the fact that the ongoing Finnish struggle was an integral part of the process of the Russian Revolution. The SWI, in other words, supported the Finnish socialist movement's struggle for national freedom because of these historical circumstances and conditions which alone lent the progressive character to this struggle. The SWI in this way adhered to a long-standing tradition of socialist internationalism which at the time lost ground within the Second International. The fulfilment as such of the demand for the right to national self-determination was postponed beyond the post-revolutionary future when the peoples living in the territories belonging to the Russian Empire each would have freed themselves from their own ruling classes. In this way the SWI cast its vote amongst other things against the 'social patriotism' attributed to the PPS.

Immediately before she had put forward the resolution on Finland, Clara Zetkin in her opening speech to the Copenhagen conference had made sure to underline that there was no place for nationalism among women.

It is our task to strengthen our work for the international dimension of the socialist movement. We have stridden through countries and come across the sea; yet when we asked from the scudding waves: 'Where are the frontiers?', they were stuck for an answer. Nature doesn't know frontiers between peoples; she remains silent there where the states have erected their boundary stakes. Socialist women in particular have compelling reasons not to tolerate *national boundaries* amongst themselves. More than men do women have an interest in building socialist society; they must want this society not only as proletarians but also in their capacity as women, as only socialism can give them full manhood. [...] We have one thing in our sight: [...] the entire emancipated

63

humanity (Standing ovations).[19]

Copenhagen was the last peace time socialist women's conference. In the anti-war resolutions and statements of the war years the demand that smaller nations too should have the right of 'self-determination and independence' – within the framework of a peace without annexations – found its place.[20]

The representational policies pursued by the SWI were characterised by a limited degree of formalisation and institutionalisation if compared to the big non-socialist international women's organisations and the Second International. There was unmistakably more clear-cut distance from the concept of national self-determination as long as it was not filled with socialist content. In addition, the SWI's conferences were especially marked by a striking absence of countries from the south-east European periphery and of non-western countries. One reason why this was so, and why there were no substantial endeavours on the part of Clara Zetkin to more visibly expand into the European periphery, was her definition of the key purposes of the SWI.

From the point of view of Zetkin, probably the most important motivation to internationalise the socialist women's movement had been from the outset to bring about the unification or co-ordination of socialist women's politics among the most important women's groups and organisations of countries considered the most weighty from the point of view of socialist politics. Upon the foundation of the SWI in 1907 suffrage and the issue of co-operation with non-socialist women's organisations were at the core of Zetkin's related endeavours. At the Copenhagen conference in 1910 the issue of gender-specific labour protection was added to the list, and again Zetkin was concerned in the first place to resolve, via internationalisation and unification, the conflicts on this topic among and within important countries and regions, especially Great Britain, Germany, Austria and Scandinavia.[21] Time and again articles in *Die Gleichheit* on the SWI, German resolutions laid before the women's conferences, and Zetkin herself in her speeches, underlined the function of the SWI as unifying the movement regarding core issues. Because the 'movements of the different countries' resembled a 'colourful sample card' of women's politics, 'continuous liaison' as embodied by the SWI was 'the prerequisite of unified systematic action in the future' and the 'commonality of practical work on the basis of a common goal'.[22]

Seen from this perspective, the inclusion and representation of comrades from smaller countries and countries from the European periphery and beyond, which might have wished to foreground issues other than the ones deemed decisive by the SWI, certainly appeared to be of limited relevance for the overall development of the organisation. The self-chosen focus of the SWI on what one might call woman-specific 'special tasks' within the large collective of international socialism added to the apparent lack of interest in enlarging the organisation so as to extend beyond its initial geographic boundaries. Taken together the principal orientation on the double goal to 'line up into one battle line the women of all countries' and to do so 'within the red International' unmistakably contributed in a manner particular to the SWI to making the core countries of European socialism the key point of reference for the organisation.[23]

War and peace in relation to international and domestic order

The political vision and the politics of peace and war were understood by many representatives of the left in international socialism as a quintessential element of their dual strategy of both challenging power relations within the international system and impacting on the relationship between international and domestic order. Under Zetkin's leadership, the SWI made the topic of peace and war into the only principal sphere of activity which did not relate directly or exclusively to the woman question or women's politics. This orientation was based not only on the leftist self-positioning within international socialism of Clara Zetkin, but also on political strategies the SWI under her leadership pursued in relation to both the Second International and (especially during wartime) non-socialist women's internationalism. This constellation of goals and the particular organisational positioning of the SWI in relation to the Second International allowed for pro-active and politically specific anti-war politics before and especially during the war.

At the time when the SWI was established, anti-war politics constituted a central and, in principle, undisputed concern of the Second International. At the Stuttgart congress of 1907 a small group of leftists within the International managed – by way of exploiting 'the limited comprehension on the part of many delegates' – to see its political key concerns included in a related resolution.[24] Leftist political analysis within international socialism constructed militarism as a key element of the politics of retaining power pursued by the great industrial states in both domestic class-specific and global imperial-colonial contexts. From this analysis emerged a particular political strategy aimed at utilising (potential) war in and between the core capitalist countries for the overthrow of the capitalist system as such by the proletarian masses. The political 'mass strike' was considered a key instrument in this regard. In 1912, at the extraordinary congress of the Second International convened in Basle, another anti-war manifesto was unanimously adopted. The Basle manifesto constructed the political position of the Second International in such a way as to keep it open to a leftist interpretation supportive of the vision of revolutionary mass politics against both war and capitalism in the event of the outbreak of hostilities between the major European powers. The price paid for this type of indeterminate unity was to dispense with any guideline as to the concrete course of action to be pursued at the outbreak of war.[25]

Against this background, in the period leading up to the First World War, internationally organised socialist women developed a politics of principled statement regarding questions of peace and war. A lead article in *Die Gleichheit* published during the international meetings at Stuttgart in 1907 took a clear political stance in matters of anti-militarism and anti-war politics. According to Zetkin it was a key task for international socialism – in the context of the tense political configuration of the time and the 'passionate controversies' to be expected at Stuttgart – 'to defang war, the ultimate and most dangerous instrument of power in the hands of the exploitative classes, and indeed to turn it into an instrument of revolution'.[26] Yet the women's conference itself was not to deal with this matter. A related motion submitted by the British Women's Labour League was passed on without discussion to the International Secretariat soon to be established.[27]

In the years after Stuttgart it became clear that Zetkin did not shy away from turning the SWI into a mouthpiece of leftist antiwar politics as pursued internationally by the group around Rosa Luxemburg. Zetkin, while using all her political leverage to support the leftist minority in international socialism, also tried to make sure the SWI proceeded with the necessary circumspection so as not to alienate from the organisation those groups and interests which did not belong to the leftist core. She tried, with mixed success, to steer a course of privileging and promoting leftwing views and groupings without alienating more moderate colleagues so as to achieve both, thus moving the socialist movement to the left whilst keeping it united.

In the early years after the foundation of the SWI, *Die Gleich-heit* regularly published articles that castigated militarism as an epiphenomenon of the politics of global inequality so distinctive of the capitalist system, without, however, pointing to the related controversy within the Second International. Militarism exclusively served those interests which were diametrically opposed to those of the proletariat. The capitalists' colonial-imperial 'greed for predation and conquest' forced the proletariat under arms against their inter-est. Financed by the taxes of the proletariat, and exclusively in support of the privileged classes back home, the bones of the sons of the German fatherland 'bleach in the swamps of China, the deserts of South West Africa'. In the domestic context militarism turned the proletarian 'in the uniform jacket' into the enemy of 'the proletarian without the coloured jacket'. In view of these facts women too had to rise against 'the "peace" bristling with guns condemning the peoples to hunger and serfdom'.[28]

On the eve of the Copenhagen women's conference of 1910, with conflict on the socialist anti-war strategy expected to erupt once again at the congress of the Second International, *Die Gleich-heit* castigated the congress programme as too limited, propagating the 'weapon of the mass-strike' instead.[29] The women's conference by acclamation passed a resolution against war and for the mainte-nance of peace. The text was designed in masterful language so as to avoid the term 'mass strike' – a combat term of the left in international socialism – and its related political tension and at the same time to attest to the strategy of direct and revolutionary action in case of any outbreak of hostilities. This double approach was at the core of the strategy pursued by the group around Zetkin in the highest echelons of the SWI. War could be prevented only through 'energetic, purposeful action of the proletariat and the victory of socialism'; the working class needed to understand that due to its role in economic life it possessed particular powers which it 'can and has to use under certain circumstances to preserve peace'.[30]

The political potential to turn the question of war and peace into the single key concern of the SWI overnight became truly manifest for the first time in 1912. Clara Zetkin in her capacity as international secretary of the SWI now made distinctive use of the informal and at the same time centralist organisational structure of the SWI in order to lend as much political substance as possible to leftist anti-war politics at the extraordinary congress of the Second International at Basle. Single-handedly she produced and distributed an appeal addressed to the women comrades of all countries calling for their participation in the congress, and she decided unilaterally to speak at the congress in the name 'of the socialist women of all countries'. Only retroactively did Zetkin ask from the members of the SWI their approval of these actions.[31] The more imperialism moved to the core of the politics of the capitalist states the more, so Zetkin argued in her Basle speech, 'war against war' moved to the core of the proletarian struggle for emancipation. '*Mass action*' involving proletarian women making up '*half of the masses*' was the order of the day.[32]

The outbreak of the First World War brought the break-up of the unity which the Second International had managed to demonstrate in its anti-war politics, at least on the surface, for many years. Against the background of the leftist self-positioning of the SWI and the special place the organisation had assigned in its political profile to the question of war and peace – it was the only non-women-specific theme it had dealt with systematically from its early days – the outbreak of the war resulted in a refocusing of all energy and political engagement towards this one field of action. As is well known to historians of the women's and workers' movements, the SWI from 1914 onwards developed into a vanguard of anti-war activism.

Only a few months after the outbreak of the war, Zetkin made clear that the time of political compromise was over and that the work of the SWI was to focus on 'one single [...] common task [...]: the work, the fight *for peace*'. As international secretary of the SWI she simply had to act. Under wartime conditions any public propaganda for peace would constitute political action. It was clear to her that she had to promote such action without the Second International, which was defunct after socialists in many countries had elected to support their nations' war efforts. At the end of 1914 the political situation was characterised, in Zetkin's view, by one single most important political tragedy, the breakdown of the International; 'the rest', so she added in a letter written in December 1914, 'is silence'.[33]

In November 1914 Zetkin addressed the SWI with an appeal for peace without annexations, which fell victim to censorship in Germany but was disseminated as a pamphlet and published in Switzerland.[34] At the same time Russian Bolshevik women had approached Zetkin with a view to initiating an unofficial international conference of leftist socialist women alone, an idea which Zetkin rejected.[35] Early in 1915, after the ISB had refused support, Zetkin together with a small group of women from several countries embarked upon preparing her own conference project. The planned conference was intended to demonstrate the political unity of internationally organised socialist women, as opposed to the Second International which was split between wartime allies and enemies. The group around Zetkin was well informed about the simultaneous preparations for the International Congress of Women at The Hague, which finally took place a month after the socialist women's conference held in Berne from 26 to 28 March 1915. The congress at The Hague brought together important representatives of non-socialist international women's organisations but also triggered the split of the IWSA and the emergence of a new important international women's organisation, the Women's International League for Peace and Freedom. The socialist women assembled at Berne formally conveyed their 'sympathy' to the upcoming congress at The Hague '[i]rrespective of the fundamental difference between the socialist and the bourgeois conceptualisation of the peace question'.[36]

While organising for the socialist women's conference Clara Zetkin did everything she could to bring together socialist women from belligerent and neutral countries.[37] The conference indeed turned out to be the first international assembly at which socialists of the belligerent countries met each other. In terms of political orientation the strategy of the group around Zetkin remained the same throughout the preparation period and the negotiations at the conference, and it was mirrored in the documents adopted by the Berne assembly. Time and again it was underlined that the fight against war was feasible only if a political mass movement was triggered here and now and that this mass movement had to be connected with the struggle for socialism. Added was the reference to the specific role of women in this development and the comparison of socialist women's steadfastness as compared to their male comrades. The latter argument was meant to support the vision of the SWI as a vanguard of a broad international peace movement of the working classes. 'That which your husbands, sons cannot yet asseverate: shall *You* proclaim it a million times' – this was the wording of the appeal addressed to the 'women of the working masses' adopted by the Berne conference.[38]

The Berne conference was organised without support from the ISB and the socialist parties of individual countries. While some of the parties openly opposed the conference, one of Zetkin's ultimate goals was to contribute to the restoration of the unity of international socialism with reference to the spirit of active anti-war policy. The main resolution passed by the women's conference identified as the key cause of war 'capitalist imperialism' and the 'need of the exploitative [...] classes in individual countries' in the course of their competition against each other to 'expand exploitation and domination beyond the boundaries of the home country'. Women were to act as the advanced guard in the fight for peace and international socialism. 'The peace-action of the socialist women must be the precursor of a general movement of the working masses for the termination of fratricide. It must serve as an important step forward towards the re-establishment of the one big workers' international.'[39] The Bolshevik minority present at the conference put on record – under the condition that its own divergent document would appear in the minutes of the conference – that 'we will not divest ourselves from joint action'.[40] Only in 1917, when the international socialist movement was breaking up into social-democratic and communist camps with accelerating speed, did the socialist internationalism of women definitely succumb to the concomitant cleavages and divisions. However, after the conflicts during the 1915 conference in Berne the Bolshevik women suspended active co-operation with the SWI.[41]

From the longer-term perspective it is obvious that in tandem with developments in international socialism, where political self-positioning regarding the question of war and peace moved to the centre of the leftist forces' quarrels with the majority, the SWI placed growing emphasis on the anti-war agenda within its overall political profile. From the outbreak of the First World War the politics of the SWI in its only remaining sphere of activity definitely departed from the developments within the disintegrated Second International. In organisational terms the wartime anti-war politics of the SWI were successful because Clara Zetkin made effective use of both the independent position of the SWI in relation to the Second International, and of its barely formalised internal structures that facilitated her centralist leadership. Historically and symbolically the Berne conference of socialist women marked an important event. The participants were united – on a rather high level of political abstraction – in their stance against unequal international power relations and overarching structures of political and economic domination in domestic and international contexts.

Conclusion

The SWI in the two spheres of activity explored in this chapter referred and related in a particular manner to particular political dynamics and inequalities on the international plane, within counries and among international movements and organisations. The process of internationalising socialist women's politics was strongly driven by hopes and endeavours of influencing and uniting through international politics – in large measure from above – the balance of political forces in socialist women's politics that to a large degree addressed genuinely national topics. Clara Zetkin and the group of leftist women socialists who joined her in bringing about the SWI and shaping its politics successfully strengthened their own political clout within international socialism and various domestic socialist movements with regard to a number of important political issues. The SWI was influential to an extent in shaping the relationships among socialist women of different countries and between socialist women and the Second International.

Struggle over representational politics did not play a similarly visible role within the history of the SWI as it did in other progressive international organisations such as the Second International and the IWSA. In the framework of a generally accepted organisational and political division of labour between the SWI and the male-dominated Second International, representational politics clearly belonged to those political fields externalised by the SWI. Together with the barely formalised and at the same time centrist leadership structures, as well as the leftist leanings of the SWI, this resulted in a characteristically multidimensional self-positioning. On the one hand the SWI was quite open to accepting representational structures which, compared to the circumstances in the pre-existing international system, enabled a rushing ahead in terms of independent and equal representation of nations (still) without a state. The SWI had this feature in common with the Second International; the same feature distinguished the organisation from more conservative non-socialist international women's organisations. Because the SWI in the field of organisational politics never specified its own rules and regulations, there was sufficient space for quick and flexible political development. On the other hand, leading representatives of the SWI were strongly committed to the idea that a right of national self-determination, if not grounded in class-specific politics and circumstances, did not exist. In its statements in favour of national self-determination the SWI – unlike the non-

socialist IWSA – never referred to pre-given constitutional arrange
ments. In the political judgement of the SWI the key point o
reference was the question whether or not national self-determina
tion in dominated territories would serve and speed up the develop
ment of the domestic and international labour movement.

This approach, which was based in leftist-socialist reasoning
distinctive of the period, informed the politics of the SWI in relation
to colonialism and imperialism as a central dimension of interna
tional inequality as well. The SWI dealt with this question largely
within the framework of its politics on peace and war. From 1914
onwards the organisation – or rather Clara Zetkin – focused exclu
sively on this sphere of activity. The leftist leanings of the leadership
of the SWI and its particular relationship with the Second Interna
tional – and to a limited degree with the IWSA – led the organisation
to develop its particular approach to anti-war politics in relation to
international, domestic and gender order. Neither male-dominated
international socialism nor the non-socialist international women's
movement was able to find a common answer to the war question
from 1914 onwards. The peace action of the SWI in terms of the
timing for the wartime conference left behind the IWSA, its inherited
competitor in the field of progressive women's politics. The wartime
anti-war politics of the SWI combined a focus on the class question
in the industrial core countries of Europe with a thorough critique
of both competition among those countries and the core industrial
countries' politics of domination overseas (but not in eastern Eu
rope).

Gender-related or women-specific considerations and argu
ments did play a limited yet visible role in the politics of internation
ally organised socialist women in relation to transnational
inequality and power relations. Because of their specific status in
the gender order proletarian women, for example, had a potential to
engage in a distinctive manner against war at the very historical
moment when their proletarian brothers were forced under arms.
They also had a particularly strong interest in socialism, which in
emancipating all humanity would do away with national boundaries
or international inequality, because as women they were denied
their full humanity in pre-socialist society.

The SWI remained white in terms of skin colour and oriented
towards the core of the international capitalist system in terms of
political geography. This was due to both the theory of social
movement dominating the organisation and its practical-political

72

ocus on unifying the socialist women's movement with regard to a number of core issues that were at the heart of conflict in socialist women's politics within and among the dominant countries of Europe. Yet this specific form of orienting towards the core, which thoroughly characterised the SWI, was not in (visible) conflict with the fact that the organisation systematically rejected and struggled against inequality in the international system as impeding social emancipation and as a political instrument blocking social emancipation. Among the international organisations dominated by white women, the SWI certainly was the only one which in the period before 1918 included such clear-cut anti-imperialism on its political agenda.

Clara Zetkin in later life

Afterword

John S Partington

As the essays contained in this collection demonstrate, there is a nebulous scholarly interest in the life, work and thought of Clara Zetkin, and yet, as these essays also show, Zetkin has largely disappeared from critical historical discourse.

During the Cold War, she was hailed in the Eastern Bloc as a heroine of the communist women's movement, and yet, beyond the symbolism of this strong woman who greeted visitors to Moscow in the 1920s and early 1930s and who founded International Women's Day (IWD), it is unclear just what was known about her at the popular level. In Wiederau and Birkenwerder, her first and her final residences in Germany, respectively, museums were created in the German Democratic Republic (GDR), and yet it is uncertain how aware people outside of these towns were of their existence. To be sure, international visitors to the GDR were taken to these places if their interests lay in the 'women's struggle', but in the great scheme of things, such celebrity introductions play little part in constructing a collective memory. During my visit to Wiederau in 2009, Ursula Bergmann, the keeper of the Zetkin museum, 'Alte Dorfschule', explained to me her bitterness when, growing up in the GDR, she was made to visit the Zetkin museum for IWD, Zetkin's birthday and other Socialist Unity Party events, when party apparatchiks would make speeches and eulogise Zetkin as a tremendous, though to the young Bergmann, non-human figure in the history of the socialist women's movement. Although such party events were tedious to all but the most loyal comrades ('Genossen' and 'Genossinnen') during the Cold War, since the fall of the Berlin Wall, Bergmann has embraced Zetkin's memory as offering distinction to the small town of Wiederau. Bergmann now appreciates some of Zetkin's achievements and is pleased to show visitors around the museum – especially those rare foreign researchers like myself, who visit Wiederau especially for that purpose.[1] What is clear is that, if Zetkin was an historic bore to the young citizens of the GDR who were force-fed a partisan historical account of her life, given the choice in democratic Germany to learn about her or ignore her, Zetkin can appeal to people in a manner which propaganda was perhaps less able to achieve.

If the damage done by the GDR regime in using Zetkin as a propaganda tool needs to be overcome through community efforts and more educative representations, the scholarly and editorial work of the GDR should not be so easily rejected. For sure, a critical attitude must be taken when approaching research produced in the GDR, but such is the case when approaching research in any society. If the GDR promoted those who promoted communism, one cannot say that it necessarily lied about its patron saints (even if certain facts, such as Zetkin's disagreements with Stalinist policy and her marriage to the social democratic artist, Friedrich Zundel, were silently ignored). Any researcher into Zetkin's career must be grateful for the wealth of material published in the GDR, such as her selected writings in three volumes or the abundance of books and pamphlets which were reprinted in East Berlin and Leipzig. The East German biographies and scholarly interpretations of Zetkin's art criticism and pedagogical notions are also valuable springboards to a fuller understanding of her achievements within and beyond the communist women's movement.[2]

If Zetkin was lauded in the East, she was virtually invisible in the West, receiving occasional denigration by historians and feminist leaders in the pre-unification Federal Republic of Germany (FRG), a victim of a conscious or subconscious ideological battle against her glorification in the GDR. Despite Zetkin's death in 1933 – sixteen years before the establishment of the GDR – FRG critics seemed unable to divorce this communist fighter for women's rights and against fascism from the communist regime which she played no part in establishing. FRG critics seemed unable to recognise the anachronism of treating Clara Zetkin as one and the same as the leaders of the GDR. Nazism, the Second World War, the Holocaust and the Cold War all contributed to making post-1945 communism a very different phenomenon to that of the pre-1933 period. Making the assumption that Zetkin would have followed the likes of Wilhelm Pieck, Walter Ulbricht and Erich Honecker as Stalinist leaders of the GDR is historically untenable, not only because of her earlier death, but also because of what we now know about her reluctance to support the Stalinisation of the Communist Party in the 1930s. But western critics, when they considered Zetkin at all, seemingly felt obliged to use her (and therefore abuse her) as a weapon against the East, and so a valuable asset to second-wave feminism was largely lost to the FRG's women's movement.[3]

Although Florence Hervé, in her essay in this collection reports little change in the German reception of Zetkin since reunification, she herself has contributed several crucial correctives to the myopic view of Clara Zetkin, and Zetkin's greater exposure in the English-language, through volumes like this one, can only add to a momentum that must surely be gathering behind her critical re-evaluation – a post-Cold War reassessment more than twenty years after the fall of the Berlin Wall. We seem to have experienced twenty years of critical stasis in regard to Zetkin, but perhaps now with a new, post-unification generation of scholars emerging, the time is ripe for a clearer understanding of Zetkin's positive contributions to the socialist movement and the women's movement, as well as a more sophisticated understanding of her flaws and political errors of judgement and tactics.

After the Second World War, Western Europe, with the support of the USA, embarked upon a project of cooperation and integration which has manifested itself in the European Union and which, since 1990, has expanded its appeal to many countries of the former Eastern Bloc. As part of this European unification – be it on a federal or a confederal basis, as the political climate at any one time dictates – a search has taken place for a common European narrative. While countries still celebrate their unique identities, there is a consensus that Europe also has a shared identity that must be explored and spread throughout the continent. Within this climate, European scholars must find a new boldness to approach figures like Clara Zetkin – figures who do not sit easily within the context of an expanding European Union, but who nonetheless made major contributions to the emergence of a transnational identity. Through such a boldness, the European narrative can continue to be constructed, though with a richer story emerging from an understanding of historical figures outside of what Zetkin would have referred to as the 'bourgeois' world.

For, despite Zetkin's rejection by the vast majority of feminists, first-wave and second, despite her demonisation by FRG critics of the Cold War, and perhaps even despite her own rhetoric, at certain points the 'proletarian' Zetkin and the 'bourgeois' 'other' come together – and it is at those points that a common ground can be found where scholars from across the political or ideological spectrum can appreciate Zetkin together, even while they will continue to disagree on and debate other aspects of her life, work and thought. In putting this collection together, Marilyn J. Boxer nd I hope to contribute to such a re-evaluation of Zetkin, which her ong career of activism fully justifies. As German academia continues to come to terms with its historical figures of the twentieth century, the English-speaking world also needs to look beyond its linguistic *cul-de-sac* to figures like Zetkin who existed almost entirely in Continental Europe (brief visits to Britain aside) but who had a significant impact on events in Britain, the USA and elsewhere.

Clara Zetkin speaking at a huge protest rally organised by the KPD (German Communist Party) on 31 August 1921 in the Berlin Lustgarten against the murder of the Reich Finance Minister Matthias Erzberger.

Glossary of Persons

Heleen Ankersmit (1869-1944): Dutch socialist, member of the Social Democratic Workers Party and secretary of the Federation of Social Democratic Women's Propaganda Clubs. She later joined the Communist Party of the Netherlands.

Louis Aragon (1897-1982): French surrealist poet, novelist and editor, a member of the PCF from 1927. He wrote *The Bells of Basel* (*Les Cloches de Bâle*, 1934), a novel featuring a character modelled on Clara Zetkin.

Inessa Armand (1874-1920): French-born Russian socialist and feminist, a member of the RSDLP from 1903. Following the Bolshevik revolution, she became director of Zhenotdel, the organisation promoting female participation in the Bolshevik Party and soviet trade unions.

Hubertine Auclert (1848-1914): French feminist and campaigner for women's suffrage, she edited *La Citoyenne* from 1881 to 1891. In 1879 she was instrumental in getting the Guesdist party (later the POF) to adopt a strong statement in favour of women's rights.

Angelica Balabanova (1878-1965): Russian socialist active in Italian socialism and the Second International, a member of the PSI from 1900, joining the Russian Bolshevik Party in 1917. Following a period as secretary of the Third International, she broke with the Bolsheviks in 1922 and returned to the PSI.

Simone de Beauvoir (1908-1986): French existentialist philosopher, social theorist and novelist, author of *The Second Sex* (1949).

August Bebel (1840-1913): German socialist leader, co-founder of the Social Democratic Workers' Party of Germany (1875, SPD from 1890), author of *Woman under Socialism* (1879).

Marthe Bigot (1878-1962): French feminist, socialist, trade unionist and teacher, contributor to several feminist journals, founder of *L'Ouvrière* and active in the PCF from 1920.

Margaret Bondfield (1873-1953): British Labour Party politician and trade unionist, the first British female cabinet minister (1929). She was an executive member of the WLL (1909-1912) and president of the TUC general council (1923).

Marie Bonnevial (1841-1918): French communard, lay teacher and co-founder of a teachers' trade union, she became a leading figure in the syndicalist movement and served as vice-president of the Ligue française pour les droits des femmes (French League for the

Rights of Women). She was the first woman to serve on the Conseil supérieur de travail (High labour council).

Lily Braun (1865-1916): German feminist and socialist, a revisionist member of the SPD. She contended for leadership of German socialist women with Zetkin, with whom she split over the issue of collaborating with 'bourgeois feminists' as well as on revisionism.

Paul Brousse (1844-1912): French anarchist activist in the First International, after moderating his views he formed the 'Possibiliste' POSR, leading its merger with several other French socialist parties to form the SFIO (1905).

Nikolai Bukharin (1888-1938): Russian Bolshevik, chair of the Third International (1926-1929) and editor of *Pravda* (1918-1929). He was purged by Joseph Stalin in the Moscow Trials of 1938.

Minna Cauer (1841-1922): educational reformer, co-editor with Lily Braun of *Die Frauenbewegung*. She was a leader of the radical German feminist movement who founded and led Frauenwohl (Women's Welfare Association) (1888-1919).

Alphonse Daudet (1840-1897): French novelist, a monarchist and anti-Semite.

Dorothea von Brandenburg (1636-1689): German princess and electress, born Dorothea Sophie von Schleswig-Holstein-Sonderburg-Glücksburg, Duke-widow of Braunschweig, Lüneburg and Celle.

Käthe Duncker (1871-1953): German social democrat from 1898 until the First World War and leader of the socialist women's movement. During the war she joined the Sparticists and became a founding member of the KPD (1918).

Felix Dzerzhinsky (1877-1926): a Polish-born revolutionary and Russian Marxist activist from 1895, he was a founding member of the SDKPiL (1899) before becoming a Bolshevik in 1917 and being appointed the first director of the soviet secret police, the Cheka (1917).

Blanche Echès (dates unknown): an otherwise unknown contributor to *L'Equité*, journal of French socialist women founded in 1913.

Friedrich Engels (1820-1895): German socialist theorist and member of the First International. He was co-author with Karl Marx of *The Communist Manifesto* (1848), editor of volumes two (1885) and three (1894) of Marx's *Capital* and author of *The Origin of the Family, Private Property and the State* (1884).

Ludovic-Oscar Frossard (1889-1946): French socialist politician, general secretary of the SFIO (1918-1920), then of the PCF (1920-1922) before rejoining the SFIO in 1923.

Jules Guesde (1845-1922): French socialist journalist and politician, a Marxist from the 1870s, he founded the POF in the early 1880s and in 1905 led it into unity with other socialist groups in the SFIO. He served as minister in the Union sacrée coalition government during the First World War.

Mathilde Guesde (née Constantin) (1843-1900): French socialist and linguist, wife of Jules Guesde. She translated Nikolay Chernyshevsky's 1863 novel *What Is To Be Done?* (*Que faire?*, 1875)

Keir Hardie (1856-1915): British socialist, trade unionist and pacifist, founder of the ILP (1893), leader of the Labour Party (1906-1908) and Labour member of Parliament.

Adolf Hitler (1889-1945): Austrian-born leader of the Nazi Party, dictator of Germany (1933-1945).

Erich Honecker (1912-1994): German socialist, member of the KPD from 1929 and of the East German SED from 1946. From 1971 he was the leader of the GDR.

Henry Mayers Hyndman (1842-1921): British socialist, founder of the Marxist SDF (1884), renamed the SDP (1908) and the BSP (1911). Taking a nationalist stance during the First World War, he led his pro-war supporters into the National Socialist Party in 1916, reverting to the name SDF in 1919.

Irina Izolskaia (dates unknown): Russian Menshevik delegate at the 1915 SWI conference in Berne, author of an article on the conference in *Nashe Slovo* - Our word - in 1915.

Jeanne d'Arc (c.1412-1431): French military leader and national patron saint, executed by the English following a succession of military victories.

Fanny Jezierska (1887-1945): Polish-born German socialist, translator of publications of the Third International, expelled from the KPD in 1929, joined the Communist Party Opposition and, later, the Socialist Workers' Party of Germany.

Marie Juchacz (1879-1956): German socialist, feminist and social reformer, appointed editor of *Die Gleichheit* following Zetkin's dismissal for her anti-war politics. She was the only woman on the committee to draft the new (Weimar) constitution and from 1920 to 1933 represented the SPD in the Reichstag.

Anna Kaminskaia (dates unknown): representative of Poland at the 1915 SWI conference in Berne.

Caroline Kauffmann (1840-1926): French radical feminist, early advocate of physical education for girls and secretary of the group la Solidarité (Solidarity). She led notorious public action modelled on the British suffragettes and supported Saumoneau's anti-war activism during the First World War.

Karl Kautsky (1854-1938): Czech-German political philosopher and socialist theorist, a leading Marxist thinker of his day. Initially a member of the Social Democratic Party of Austria in 1875, he joined the SPD in exile in the 1880s, though split with them over involvement in the First World War. He joined the USPD in 1917 before rejoining the SPD in 1920. From 1883 to 1917, he edited the influential theoretical socialist journal, *Die Neue Zeit*.

Helmut Kohl (born 1930): German Christian democratic politician, Chancellor of the FRG from 1982 to 1998.

Alexandra Kollontai (1872-1952): Russian socialist revolutionary, joining the RSDLP in 1899 and following the Menshevik tendency before joining the Bolsheviks in 1914. She became the first woman government minister when appointed People's Commissar for Social Welfare in 1917, establishing the Zhenotdel in 1919. She was also the first female ambassador, when she was appointed to Norway in 1923. She was a member of the Workers' Opposition in the early 1920s, before it was crushed by soviet authorities.

Nadezhda Krupskaya (1869-1939): Russian revolutionary, wife of V.I. Lenin, a Bolshevik who held various education posts in the soviet government during the 1920s and 1930s.

Paul Lafargue (1842-1911): Cuban-born French socialist revolutionary and writer, husband of Karl Marx's daughter, Laura. Initially an anarchist in the First International, he shifted to revolutionary socialism and became a leader of the POF from 1882. When that party merged into the SFIO, a decision he opposed, he largely withdrew from public political life. He wrote *La Question de la femme* (The woman question, 1904).

Vladimir Il'ich Lenin (1870-1924): Russian revolutionary, leader of the Bolshevik faction of the RSDLP which successfully took power in Russia during the 1917 revolution, forming the Soviet Union in 1922, which he led until his death.

Karl Liebknecht (1871-1919): German social democrat and founding member of the KPD. The first SPD parliamentarian to oppose the First World War, he helped form the Spartacus League which rose in revolution in 1918. He was murdered, along with Rosa Luxem-

burg, during the crushing of the German revolution by the firs
postwar SPD government.

Zlata Ionovna Lilina (pseudo. Zinaida Evnovna Bernshtein) (1882
1929): Russian Bolshevik, wife of Grigorii Zinoviev, present at the
1915 SWI conference in Berne; active in educational reform ir
Soviet Russia.

Mary Longman (dates unknown): poor law investigator, membe
(from 1910) and general secretary (1915-1916) of the WLL, Britisl
delegate to the 1915 SWI conference in Berne.

Charles Longuet (1839-1903): Communard, journalist, Proudhon
ist member of the First International, later a Marxist, husband o
Karl Marx's daughter, Jenny.

Rosa Luxemburg (1871-1919): Polish-born socialist revolutionar;
and theorist, founding member of the SDKPiL and leader in the SPI
and the USPD. She co-founded the KPD (1918), and was murderec
in January 1919, during the unsuccessful German 'Spartacist
Revolution.

Mary Macpherson (dates unknown): founding secretary of the WLl
(1906-1910), secretary of the Railway Women's Guild, and Britisl
delegate to the 1907 SWI conference in Stuttgart.

Benoît Malon (1841-1893): Communard, member of the Firs
International, worker, later journalist, early advocate of unificatior
of French socialist parties.

Eleanor Marx (1855-1898): British-born youngest daughter of Kar
Marx, active in socialist movements from an early age. She helpec
organise British trade unions, translated political and literary work;
and served as translator at congresses of the Second International

Jenny Marx (1844-1883): eldest daughter of Karl Marx, wrote fo;
the socialist press. Married to French Communard, Charles Longuet

Karl Marx (1818-1883): German socialist and revolutionary, autho;
of *Capital* (1867-1894) and co-author, with Friedrich Engels, of *Th*
Communist Manifesto (1848). In 1864 he formed the Internationa
Workingmen's Association, or First International.

Laura Marx Lafargue (1845-1911): Belgian-born middle daughte;
of Karl Marx, married to Paul Lafargue. She translated works o
Marx and Friedrich Engels into French and participated in con
gresses of the Second International.

Guy de Maupassant (1850-1893): French novelist and short story
writer.

Louise Michel (1830-1905): heroine of the Paris Commune of 1871
famous for her defiance of court-martial which led to her exile ir

New Caledonia. After the general amnesty of 1880, she was an active propagandist for anarchism and socialism.

Dora Montefiore (1851-1933): British-Australian suffragist and socialist, after membership in the Women's Social and Political Union, she joined the SDF and advocated universal adult suffrage. She was a founding member of the CPGB, and also represented the Australian party in Moscow in 1924.

Louise Otto-Peters (1819-1895): German writer and founder after the revolution of 1848 of a newspaper dedicated to women's rights; co-founder with (Zetkin's early teacher) Auguste Schmidt of the General Union of German Women. She is considered the founder of German liberal feminism, an early influence on August Bebel.

Sylvia Pankhurst (1882-1960): British suffragette, communist and anti-fascist, after breaking with the Women's Social and Political Union (1914), she led the East London Federation of Suffragettes and founded the Communist Party (British Section of the Third International) in 1920. She broke with Lenin over parliamentarism and withdrew from communist politics in the early 1920s.

Cedar Paul (died 1972): British socialist and journalist, member of the WLL, the ILP (1912-1919) and secretary of the British section of the SWI (1917-1919). She joined the CPGB in 1919.

Madeleine Pelletier (1874-1939): first female medical doctor allowed to practice in mental hospitals in France, famous as a cross-dressing radical feminist advocating public violence against property modelled on the British suffragettes. Author of over forty works of philosophy and politics, she held positions of leadership in several socialist groups. She was delegated to seven SFIO national congresses and to the Stuttgart meeting of the SWI (1907).

Comrade Perlmutter (dates unknown): an otherwise unknown Polish delegate to the 1910 SWI conference in Copenhagen.

Marion Phillips (1881-1932): Australian-born British socialist, member (1908-1918) and secretary (1912-1918) of the WLL, editor of the *League Leaflet* and *Labour Woman* and secretary of the Labour Party's Women's Section (1918-1932). She was Labour MP for Sunderland (1929-1931).

Wilhelm Pieck (1876-1960): German socialist, member of the SPD (1895-1918), the KPD (1918-1946) and the SED (1946-1960). He was the general secretary of the Third International (1938-1943) and president of the GDR (1949-1960).

Charles Rappoport (1865-1941): Russian-born French socialist, journalist and writer, he supported joining the Third International at Tours and participated in founding the PCF, which he left in 1938. He was a neighbour of Zetkin during her Paris exile and her life-long friend and admirer.

Marianne Rauze (1875-1959): French socialist and feminist, founder in 1913 of socialist women's journal, *L'Equité*, fought unsuccessfully against Louise Saumoneau to broaden membership of the socialist women's group to include non-party members. From a military family, she supported the First World War and opposed French participation in the SWI conference in Berne. She later became a pacifist.

Henrietta Roland Holst (1869-1952): Dutch Marxist and international socialist leader, she was a supporter of Lenin and a follower of Zetkin in hostility to non-socialist feminists. She was active in the Zimmerwald left, and was also known for her literary work which includes a biography of Rosa Luxemburg.

Elena Rozmirovich (1886-1953): Bolshevik underground agent and journalist, attended international socialist conferences at Basle and Berne, held numerous Communist Party posts.

Ada Salter (1866-1942): British Christian socialist, member of the ILP and the WLL (from 1908), she was the first female councillor to be elected in London (1910).

Louise Saumoneau (1875-1949): seamstress, teacher, and cofounder in 1899 of the first group of French socialist women. She was a follower of Zetkin, founder, editor and publisher of the long-lived journal, *La Femme socialiste*. She was active in the SFIO and, briefly, in the Third International.

Friedrich Schiller (1759-1805): German poet, philosopher, historian and playwright.

Ida Schmidt (dates unknown): otherwise unknown Swiss socialist involved with the organisation of the Extraordinary International Socialist Peace Congress in Basle in 1912.

Marcel Sembat (1862-1922): socialist, lawyer, journalist, deputy and an adherent of the Socialist Revolutionary Party (a Blanquist party led by Edouard Vaillant). He became a minister in the wartime coalition government and voted at the Tours congress against joining the Third International.

Toni (Sidonie) Sender (1888-1964): German socialist, a representative of the USPD, then the SPD, in the Reichstag, 1920-1933. She joined the socialist movement in Paris, returned to Germany when the First World War began, broke with the SPD over its support for ar, attended 1915 SWI conference in Berne; emigrated to the USA fter 1933 and was later active in United Nations.

oseph Stalin (1878-1953): Georgian-born Russian Bolshevik, ader of the Soviet Union from c. 1927 to 1953.

lena Stasova (1873-1966): Russian socialist, member of the SDLP from 1898, following the Bolshevik tendency from 1903. She ecame the party's secretary and held important positions in the hird International.

elene Stöcker (1869-1943): German radical feminist, pacifist, exual reformer, co-founder of the League for the Protection of others (Bund für Mutterschutz).

akov Sverdlov (1885-1919): Russian socialist revolutionary, he ined the RSDLP in 1902, joining the Bolshevik faction the follow- ng year. During the Bolshevik revolution, he was the architect of he Red Terror.

ertha Thalheimer (1883-1959): German member of the SPD who ined the Spartacus group and later the KPD, attended the Zim- erwald conference.

onette Thomas (dates unknown): French socialist, suffragist and dvocate of gender parity in the legislature, she was a pacifist in the irst World War, and remained active in the interwar period, writing r *La Voix des femmes* and *Le Populaire*.

hucydides (c. 460 BC-c. 395 BC): ancient Greek historian, most oted for his history of the wars between Sparta and Athens.

eo Tolstoy (1828-1910): Russian anarchist, novelist and short ory writer.

eon Trotsky (1879-1940): Russian revolutionary, member of the SDLP, he initially joined the Menshevik faction of the party before ecoming a Bolshevik in 1917. He created the Red Army during the ussian Civil War.

alter Ulbricht (1893-1973): German socialist, member of the SPD 912-1917), the USPD (1917-1920), the KPD (1920-1946) and the ED (1946-1973). He was the effective leader of the GDR from 1950 1971.

douard Vaillant (1840-1915): French socialist and communard, ter elected deputy, leader of the Socialist Revolutionary 3lanquist) Party until joining the unified SFIO.

line Valette (1850-1899): leader of French socialist and feminist ovements, secretary of the National Council of the POF and of the rench Federation of Feminist Groups. Vocational teacher, journal-

ist and women's labour inspector, she co-authored *Socialisme* ∢
sexualisme (1893).

Varvara (dates unknown): an otherwise unknown Russian schoⲟ
friend of Clara Zetkin in Leipzig who accompanied her on a trip t
Russia in the 1870s.

Charles Vérecque (1872-1933): French socialist and journalis￭
close ally of Jules Guesde in the POF.

William English Walling (1877-1936): American socialist and civ￭
rights activist, he resigned from the Socialist Party of America i
1917 over the party's anti-war position.

Wilhelm II (1859-1941): German emperor (1888-1918).

Comrade Wilkominski (dates unknown): an otherwise unknow￭
Polish delegate to the 1910 International Socialist Congress i￭
Copenhagen.

Zenaida Yusupov (1861-1939): Russian princess, last private res
dent of the Yusupov Palace which became the Ministry of Educatioⲟ
following the Bolshevik revolution.

Clara Zetkin (1857-1933): German socialist, member of the SPⰊ
(1878-1917), the USPD (1917-1920) and the KPD (1920-1933). Sⱨ
edited *Die Gleichheit* (1892-1917) and founded the SWI (1907).

Konstantin 'Kostia' Zetkin (1885-1980): younger son of Clara an￭
Ossip Zetkin, became a physician, member of the Frankfurt Schoⲟ
for Social Research. After the Second World War, he emigrated t
USA and later to Canada.

Maxim Zetkin (1883-1965): elder son of Clara Zetkin and Ossi￭
Zetkin, worked on *Die Gleichheit*, became a physician, practiced i
Moscow and in the Soviet Zone of Berlin, later professor at Berlin
Humboldt University.

Ossip Zetkin (1850-1889): Russian revolutionary and journalis￭
partner of Clara Zetkin.

Louise Zietz (1865-1922): German socialist and journalist, sⱨ
joined Zetkin in opposing the First World War. She was expelle￭
from the SPD executive committee, though later elected a socialis￭
deputy to the Reichstag.

Grigorii Zinoviev (1883-1936): Russian Bolshevik, active in tⱨ
1905 revolution. Together with Lenin, he led the Zimmerwald lef￭
He was chair of Executive Committee of the Third International an￭
a supporter of Trotsky. He was executed in 1936 during a Stalinis￭
purge.

Emile Zola (1840-1902): French novelist and civil rights campaigne￭

Friedrich Zundel (1875-1948): German social democrat and artis￭
husband of Clara Zetkin.

Notes on Contributors

Marilyn J. Boxer is a professor emerita of history at San Francisco State University, USA. Her publications include 'Socialism Faces Feminism: The failure of synthesis in France, 1879-1914', in *Socialist Women: European Socialist Feminism in the Late Nineteenth and Early Twentieth Centuries*, ed. Marilyn J. Boxer and Jean H. Quaaert (New York, 1978), 'Rethinking the Socialist Construction and International Career of the Concept "Bourgeois Feminism"', *American Historical Review* (2007), and 'Linking Socialism, Feminism, and Social Darwinism in Belle Epoque France: The maternalist politics and journalism of Aline Valette', *Women's History Review* (2012). She is also author of *When Women Ask the Questions: Creating women's studies in America* (Baltimore, MD, 1998 pb 2001).

Florence Hervé received her doctorate in German studies in Paris and works as a journalist, author and lecturer. She is the co-editor of the 'agenda wir frauen' and of the feminist review *wir frauen*. She has published innumerable books, including biographies, dictionaries, women's histories and illustrated works. She has published widely on Clara Zetkin, including *Clara Zetkin oder: Dort kämpfen, wo das Leben ist*, 2nd edn (Berlin, 2011). In 2011 she was awarded the Clara Zetkin Women's Prize of the Links Partei.

Natalia Novikova is a senior lecturer at the Department of History, Yaroslavl State Pedagogical University, Russia, where she also completed her doctorate in modern history. As a postdoctoral fellow at the Institute of Ethnology and Anthropology of the Russian Academy of Science, Moscow, she is currently working on a project entitled 'The Problem of National Culture and National Identity in Women's Movements in the Early 20th Century: British and Russian Cases'.

John S. Partington received his doctorate from the University of Reading, UK. He has published six books, including *Building Cosmopolis: The Political Thought of H. G. Wells* (Aldershot, 2003), *The Reception of H. G. Wells in Europe* (with Patrick Parrinder, London, 2005, pb 2013), *H.G. Wells in Nature, 1893-1946: A Reception Reader* (Frankfurt, 2008) and *The Life, Music and Thought of Woody Guthrie: A Critical Appraisal* (Farnham, 2011). He has published essays on Phoebe Cusden and Lorenzo Quelch in the *Dictionary of Labour Biography* (vol.13, Basingstoke, 2010) and has written a comparative essay on the socialisms of George Orwell and H. G. Wells (*Journal of Contemporary History*, January 2004). He is currently researching the reception and influence of Clara Zetkin in British politics, 1886 to 1933.

Susan Zimmermann is a professor of history at Central European University, Budapest, Hungary. Her current research is on the involvement of international labour and women's policy in relation to global inequalities of power and social position and the changing relationships between class, 'race' and gender in international politics in the first half of the 20th century. She has recently published a monograph, *GrenzÜberschreitungen. Internationale Netzwerke, Organisationen, Bewegungen und die Politik der globalen Ungleichheit vom 17. bis zum 21. Jahrhundert* (Vienna, 2010).

Clara Zetkin as depicted on an International
Women's Day poster from 1960.

Endnotes

Introduction

1. Cf. Gilbert Badia, *Clara Zetkin: Féministe sans frontières* (Paris, 1993), p.9; and Richard J. Evans, *The Feminists: Women's Emancipation Movements in Europe, America and Australasia, 1840-1920* London, 1977), p.161.

2. For the various biographies published in Germany and France, see Florence Hervé's chapter.

3. See, for example, a tribute to IWD by a Thornhill, Ontario, high school that describes the Copenhagen conference as a meeting of working women' and omits any reference to its founder as a socialist. See *St Elizabeth's Catholic High School Newsletter*, 1 (April 2011), p.5. Commercialisation of the event can be seen in the 39 different IWD greeting cards shown at www.greetingcarduniverse.com. Trivialisation of IWD can also be seen in Russia, where in a recent English-language magazine for tourists, the 'Letter from the Publisher' by John Ortega offers readers (implicitly male) a reminder to buy flowers for women on 8 March, p.2, and a feature story on IWD traces its history to 'Klara Tsetkin', noting that 'it has long lost its political meaning' and exists today as an occasion for men to 'show appreciation for the women in their lives'. See Elena Rubinova, 'The 8th of March: A truly significant holiday', *Passport* (March 2009), p.12.

4. Susan Zimmermann, 'A struggle over gender, class and the vote: unequal international interaction and the birth of the "Female International" of socialist women (1905-1907)', in Oliver Janz and Daniel Schönpflug, eds, *Gender History in a Transnational Perspective* (New York, forthcoming). The term 'unisexual' is borrowed from Caroline Kauffmann and Dr Madeleine Pelletier, French socialist feminists who posted flyers around Paris calling for 'universal suffrage, not unisexual suffrage'. See Marilyn J Boxer, 'Socialism faces feminism in France: The failure of synthesis in France, 1879-1914', in Marilyn J Boxer and Jean H Quataert, eds, *Socialist Women: European socialist feminism in the nineteenth and early twentieth centuries* (New York, 1978), pp.75-111 p.125). Pelletier was a delegate to the Stuttgart conference of 1907.

5. For Zetkin's experience of 'international proletarian solidarity in her own life', see Luise Dornemann, *Clara Zetkin: Ein Lebensbild* (Berlin, 1960), pp.56-61.

6. J P Nettl, *Rosa Luxemburg*, abr. ed. (Oxford, 1969), p.6. For a sense of how close the friendship was, see the many letters from Luxemburg

to Zetkin in *The Letters of Rosa Luxemburg*, ed. Georg Adler, Peter Hudis, and Annelies Laschitza, tr. George Shriver (London and New York, 2011). The last letter Luxemburg wrote, four days before her murder, was addressed to 'Dearest Klara' (pp.490-493) and she signed most of her letters to Zetkin with 'a thousand embraces', 'kisses from the heart' and similar phrases.

7. Nettl, *Rosa Luxemburg*, p.418.

8. According to Zetkin, by May 1915 some 100,000 copies had been distributed in forty locales; by July, 300,000 had appeared in 100 places. See Badia, *Clara Zetkin*, pp.155, 157.

9. 'The First Women's Club', *Azerbaijan Gender Information Center*, http://www.gender-az.org/index_en.shtml?id_doc=189 (accessed 10 July 2011).

10. Zetkin, letter to her son Maxim, 10 November 1921, in Clara Zetkin, *Batailles pour les femmes*, ed. Gilbert Badia, et al. (Paris, 1980), p.58.

11. For widespread inspiration, see, for example, Zetkin's impact on American women, in Sally M Miller, 'Women in the party bureaucracy: Subservient functionaries', in Sally M Miller, ed., *Flawed Liberation. Socialism and feminism* (Westport, Conn., 1981), pp.13-35. For a contemporary example, see Elena Linarez on the Mouvement des femmes Clara Zetkin in Venezuela at http://solidarite-internationale-pcf.over-blog.net/article-clara-zetkin-et-la-lutte-ideologique-par-elena-linarez-presidente-du-mouvement-des-femmes-communistes-clara-zetkin-au-venezuela-54195299.html (accessed 30 July 2011).

12. On Zetkin's stance regarding non-socialist feminism, see Marilyn J Boxer, 'Rethinking the socialist construction and international career of the construct "bourgeois feminism"', *American Historical Review*, 112 (2007), pp.131-158.

13. Florence Hervé, 'In Frankreich geschätzt, in der Bundesrepublik diffamiert? Erfahrungen mit der Rezeption von Clara Zetkin', in *'Ich kann nicht gegen meine Überzeugung handeln': Clara Zetkin zum 150. Geburtstag*, ed. Astrid Franzke and Ilse Nagelschmidt (Leipzig, 2008), pp.105-116; and Florence Hervé, 'Vilipendée à l'ouest, encensée à l'est? Autour de la réception de Clara Zetkin à l'occasion de son 150ième anniversaire', *Allemagne d'aujourd'hui*, 181 (September 2007), pp.148-152.

Chapter One

1. An earlier version of this essay was presented at the conference of the International Federation for Research in Women's History during the 21st International Congress of Historical Sciences in Amsterdam in August 2010.

2. Florence Hervé, 'Geliebt und gehässt: Clara Zetkin', in Hervé, *Clara Zetkin oder: Dort kämpfen, wo das Leben ist* (Berlin, 2007), pp.7-37; Hervé, 'In Frankreich geschätzt, in der Bundesrepublik diffamiert? Erfahrungen mit der Rezeption von Clara Zetkin', in *'Ich kann nicht gegen meine Überzeugung handeln': Clara Zetkin zum 150. Geburtstag*, ed. Astrid Franzke and Ilse Nagelschmidt (Leipzig, 2008), pp.105-116; Gilbert Badia and Florence Hervé, 'Einige Bemerkungen zur Biographie von Tânia Puschnerat über Clara Zetkin', *junge Welt*, 7/8 (August 2004), p.6; and Puschnerat's email to John S Partington, 6 December 2009, declaring that her thesis about Zetkin's authoritarian character had 'not been proved false'. See also Gilbert Badia, *Clara Zetkin: Féministe sans frontières* (Paris, 1993); on Zetkin's public refusal to term herself a feminist, see below.

3. Police report dated 22 September 1882 indicating Zetkin had 'just arrived' in Paris; Archives de la préfecture de police (APP) B/A 1301. Biographies include Gertrud G.L. Alexander, *Aus Clara Zetkins Leben und Werk* (Berlin, 1927); Wilhelm Pieck, *Clara Zetkin: Leben und Kampf* (Berlin, 1948); Luise Dornemann, *Clara Zetkin; Ein Lebensbild* (Berlin, 1960); Karen Honeycutt, 'Clara Zetkin: A left-wing socialist and feminist in Wilhelmian Germany', unpublished doctoral dissertation (Columbia University, 1975); Badia, *Clara Zetkin*; Tânia Puschnerat, *Clara Zetkin: Bürgerlichkeit und Marxismus: Eine Biographie* (Essen, 2003); Tânia Unlüdag-Puschnerat, 'A German Communist: Clara Zetkin (1857-1933), in *Agents of the Revolution: New biographical approaches to the history of international communism in the age of Lenin and Stalin*, ed. Kevin Morgan, Gidon Cohen and Andrew Flinn (Oxford, 2005), pp.93-110.

4. For 'decisive years', see Badia, *Féministe sans frontières*, p.23; for proletarian experience, see Dornemann, *Clara Zetkin*, pp.59-60. This period is also recalled by Charles Rappoport in *Une Vie révolutionnaire 1883-1940: Les mémoires de Charles Rappoport*, ed. Marc Lagana (Paris, 1991), pp.108-111. Rappoport, a Russian émigré who was Zetkin's Paris neighbour and lifelong friend, visited her in Stuttgart in 1910 and was instrumental in arranging her trip to Tours in December 1920.

5. She also met Karl Marx's son-in-law, the Communard Charles Longuet (whose wife, Jenny Marx, died soon after Zetkin's arrival in

91

Paris), and the youngest Marx daughter, Eleanor, with whom she shared translating duties at socialist conferences. The Lafargues assist ed during Ossip's illness by sharing their domestic help; see Anne Lopes and Gary Roth, *Men's Feminism: August Bebel and the German socialist movement* (Amherst, New York, 2000), p.211. On hunger, horsemeat wound, see Dornemann, *Clara Zetkin*, pp.59-66. Claude Willard reports assistance in reverse, provided by Zetkin to Mathilde Guesde when the French leader's wife lacked money for food; see Claude Willard, *Les Guesdistes: Le Mouvement socialiste en France (1893-1905)* (Paris 1965), p.78.

6. Puschnerat, *Clara Zetkin*, p.48. Police reported that the Zetkins depended on subsidies from Germany, Russia and Switzerland; APP B/A 1301, 6 September 1886.

7. Clara Zetkin, 'Louise Michel nach ihren Memoiren', *Die Neue Zeit*, 4 (1886), pp.210-221. By 1890 she had published fourteen biographical pieces; see Katja Haferkorn, 'Clara Zetkin in Paris (1882-1890)', *Bei träge zur Geschichte der Arbeiterbewegung*, 26.2 (1984), pp.184-196 (p.189). On Clara's authorship of 'character sketches' published under the name of Ossip, see Marie-Louise Goergen, 'Paris, Un Lieu de Rencontre pour les Socialistes Allemands et Français avant 1914', in *Deutsche Handwerker, Arbeiter und Dienstmädchen in Paris: Eine ver gessene Migration im 19 Jahrhundert*, ed. Mareike König (Munich, 2003), p.187. Fritz Staude places Zetkin's first publication in German on 1 January 1885, in *Der Sozialdemokrat*, on 'Die Sozial-demokratie und die Frauenarbeit'; Staude, 'Die Bedeutung der Jahre der Pariser Emigration für Clara Zetkins Entwicklung', *Mitteilungsblatt der Forsc hungsgemeinschaft*, 'Geschichte des Kampfes der Arbeitersklasse um die Befreiung der Frau', 2 (1983), p.10. Honeycutt states that Zetkin's first article on the 'woman question' appeared under her first name only, as 'Les femmes comme inventriées', *Le Socialiste*, 12 February 1887; Honeycutt, 'Clara Zetkin', p.70, n.81.

8. Fritz Staude, 'Clara Zetkin's Weg zum proletarischen International-ismus', in *Clara Zetkin Kolloqium der Forschungsgemeinschaft*, 'Geschichte des kampfes der Arbeiterklasse um die Befreiung der Frau', Leipzig (1978), pp.24-34 (p.29).

9. Dornemann, *Clara Zetkin*, pp.66-67; Haferkorn, 'Clara Zetkin in Paris', p.185; Honeycutt, 'Clara Zetkin', p.64.

10. *Le Socialiste*, 12 February 1887.

11. *Le Socialiste*, 5 March 1887.

12. Badia, *Féministe sans frontières*, p.34. Between 30 July 1887 and 19 December 1891 Clara herself wrote more than 125 essays; Fritz Staude, 'Clara Zetkin über der Anarchismus in Frankreich', *Mitteilungs-

blatt der Forschungsgemeinschaft, 'Geschichte des Kampfes der Arbeitersklasse um die Befreiung der Frau', 1 (1982), pp.12-15 (p.12).

13. On organising committee, chaired by Paul Lafargue, and speech, see Dornemann, *Clara Zetkin*, pp.79-88.

14. Ellen Carol Dubois, 'Woman Suffrage and the Left: An international socialist-feminist perspective', *New Left Review*, 1.186 (1991), pp.20-45 (p.29).

15. For Eleanor Marx and Zetkin as translators at the 1896 London meeting of the Second International, see Yvonne Kapp, *Eleanor Marx*, vol.2 (New York, 1972), p.658, n.3.

16. On Zetkin's international outreach, see her 1910 letter to Sweden reporting contacts in European countries and the USA; www.arbark/se (accessed 23 September 2010).

17. On Braun, see Jean H. Quataert, *Reluctant Feminists in German Social Democracy, 1885-1917* (Princeton, 1979), pp.113-129.

18. Charles Sowerwine, 'The Organisation of French Socialist Women, 1880-1914: A European perspective for women's movements', *Historical Reflections/Réflexions historiques*, 3 (1976), pp.3-24 (p.7).

19. On the SWI, see Susan Zimmermann, 'A struggle over gender, class and the vote: unequal international interaction and the birth of the "Female International" of socialist women (1905-1907)', in *Gender History in a Transnational Perspective*, ed. Oliver Janz and Daniel Schönpflug (New York, forthcoming).

20. For the text of the resolution, see Philip S Foner, ed., *Clara Zetkin, Selected writings* (New York, 1984), p.108.

21. On 'preparatory work', see Zetkin's letter to Karl Liebknecht, *Bolshevik*, 13/14 (1934), pp.104-107, quoted in Olga Hess Gankin and H H Fisher, *The Bolsheviks and the World War: The origin of the Third International* (Stanford, 1940), p.287. This volume includes an unofficial account of and texts from the Berne conference, and a count of delegates from France (one), Germany (seven), England (four), Switzerland (two), the Netherlands (three), Italy (one), Poland (one) and Russia (six). On the informal meeting at Stockholm, see Gankin and Fisher, *The Bolsheviks*, pp.297, 688-691. For a detailed account by an Englishwoman at Berne, see Marion Phillips, 'The Women's International', *Contemporary Review*, 593 (May 1915), pp.646-651.

22. For Zetkin's acceptance of class collaboration with 'bourgeois nationalist' women, see Zetkin, 'The Duty of Women in War-Time', *Justice*, 19 November 1914, p.2. See also Zetkin, 'Internationale Solidarität und Friedenwille der Frauen alles Länder', *Die Gleichheit*, 22 January 1915.

23. On the planned 1919 meeting, see Robert Wheeler, 'German Women and the Communist International: The case of the Independent Social Democrats', *Central European History*, 8 (1975), pp.113-139 (p.118 n.15).

24. *L'Equité*, 15 March 1914 and 1 April 1914.

25. On Zetkin's views, see Edmond Peluso, 'Ce que pense Clara Zetkin du mouvement des femmes socialistes en France', *L'Humanité*, 13 March 1913.

26. For Vérecque, see 'Notes et souvenirs', *La Femme socialiste*, October 1932. For Zetkin's acceptance speech, minus the statement that Vérecque lamented, see *Compte rendu sténographique non officiel de la version française du cinquième congrès socialiste international tenu à Paris du 23 au 27 septembre 1900* (Paris, 1901), p.186.

27. Pelletier, *La Fronde*, 1 September 1904; Echès, *L'Equité*, 15 October 1913; Rauze, *La Vague*, 2 (14 August 1919). Zetkin watched developments in France and sent letters of counsel, appreciation or regret; e.g., a note on Aline Valette's passing, in *Le Socialiste*, 9 (April 1899); and praise for a socialist women's demonstration in Paris, in 'Our Sisters Abroad', *Labour Woman*, 1.12 (April 1914).

28. On Saumoneau's influencing French socialist women away from feminism and her control of attempts to found separate socialist women's organisations, see Sowerine, 'Organisation of French Socialist Women', p.7; Bard, *Un Siècle d'antiféminisme* ([Paris], 1999), p.16.

29. Charles Sowerwine, *Sisters or Citizens: Women and socialism in France since 1876* (Cambridge, 1982), pp.136-138.

30. In a letter of 3 December 1914 to Heleen Ankersmit, Zetkin asked the Dutch comrade to republish her appeal and transmit it to Britain and Belgium; she 'hoped to convey the appeal to the French women by another route'; 'Letter to Heleen Ankersmit', in Foner, ed., *Clara Zetkin*, pp.116-29 (p.126).

31. Louise Saumoneau, *Les Femmes socialistes contre la guerre. III. Avant l'Appel de Clara Zetkin* (Paris, 1923), p.7. For a list of antiwar circulars published and diffused by Saumoneau, see Aude Sowerwine and Charles Sowerwine, eds, *Le Mouvement ouvrier français contre la guerre, 1914-1918: Textes et documents*, vol.2 (Paris,1985).

32. Numerous accounts of these events include a detailed report by Sowerwine, *Sisters or Citizens*. For Zetkin's appreciation of Frenchwomen and others who spread her appeal, see 'Internationale Solidarität und Friedenswille der Frauen aller Länder', *Die Gleichheit*, 22 January 1915.

33. Saumoneau describes her arrest and seven-week confinement in *La Femme socialiste*, 33-34 (November-December 1915).

34. One observer saw the Berne meeting as an 'effort at German penetration by means of feminism [that] failed; the international weapon was broken by French women'; Marie de la Hire, *La Femme française: Son activité pendant la guerre* (Paris, 1917), p.298.

35. On refusal, see *La femme socialiste*, 5 (new series) (1948).

36. 'Pour une Internationale d'action', *La Femme socialiste*, 3.2 (April 1919).

37. *La Femme socialiste*, 4.87 (September 1930).

38. For the Zetkin obituary, see *La Femme socialiste*, 124 (October 1933). According to the writer (probably Saumoneau), 'aged and blind, she lived until her death in Russia, where she was kept like a prisoner and allowed freedom only on occasion, to attend sessions of the German Reichstag'.

39. Saumoneau, following a brief membership, was excluded by action of the Third International for a 'severe' breach of discipline when she defied the Seine Federation to present her own list of candidates for its executive committee; *La Vie ouvrière*, 23 April 1920.

40. *Le Populaire*, 2 December 1918, 10 December 1918, 6 January 1919.

41. For example, in French journals Zetkin was portrayed visually more positively than other German socialists; Goergen, 'Paris, Un lieu de rencontre', pp.173-174.

42. Badia, *Féministe sans frontières*, p.7.

43. *Le Populaire*, 30 December 1920.

44. *New York Times*, 29 December 1920; Annie Kriegel, *Le Congrès de Tours (décembre 1920): Naissance du parti communiste français* (Paris, 1964), p.183; Georges LeFranc, *Le Mouvement socialiste dans la Troisième République* (Paris, 1963), pp.236-237. For a sympathetic contemporary account, see Dora B Montefiore, 'History in the Making: The Congress of the French Socialist Party at Tours', *The Communist*, 6 January 1921, p.5, rpt in *Marxist Internet Archive* (2007), http://Marxists.catbull.com/archive/montefiore/ (accessed 6 March 2010). Other accounts include Patricia van der Esch, *Le Deuxième Internationale, 1889-1923* (Paris, 1957), p.156, who writes that Zetkin poured oil on the fire'; Jean Fréville, *Né du Feu: De la faillité de la IIe Internationale au congrès de Tours* (Paris, 1960), and Fréville, *La Nuit finit à Tours: Naissance du Parti Communiste français* (Paris, 1970). For a documentary record and full text of Zetkin's telegram and speech, see Jean Charles, et al., eds, *Le Congrès de Tours (18e Congrès national du*

Parti socialiste) – texte intégral (Paris, 1980). The speech appeared in *L'Humanité*, 29 December 1920.

45. *Le Populaire*, 30 December 1920; Rappoport, *Une Vie révolution naire*, p.368, n.258. For Zetkin's view of proceedings and implicit criticism of Zinoviev, see her letter to Lenin, 25 January 1921, *Revolutionary History*, 9.2 (n.d.), pp.217-222.

46. *Le Populaire*, 30 December 1920; *L'Humanité*, 29 December 1920 *New York Times*, 29 December and 31 December 1920.

47. Charles, et al., eds, *Le Congrès de Tours*, p.74.

48. *La Vie ouvrière*, 18 June 1919, 22 October 1919; *La Femme social iste*, 3 (10 July 1920), (15 July 1920) and (1 August 1920).

49. Wheeler, 'German Women and the Communist International' p.132, n.70.

50. Sowerwine, *Sisters or Citizens?* p.165.

51. Ibid., pp.173-174.

52. Bard, *Les Filles de Marianne*, p.345.

53. For Zetkin's complaint about her 'solitary confinement' in a letter of September 1931, see Ünlüdag-Puschnerat, 'Clara Zetkin: A German Communist', p.96. Puschnerat likens Zetkin's celebrity in her later years to a 'saint's cult'. See Ünlüdag-Puschnerat, 'Clara Zetkin: A German Communist', p.94.

54. Marilyn J Boxer, 'Rethinking the Socialist Construction and Inter national Career of the Construct "Bourgeois Feminism"', *American Historical Review*, 112.1 (2007), pp.131-158.

55. Klara Zetkin, *Lenin on the 'Woman Question'* (New York, [1934]).

56. For bias, see Elaine Marks and Isabelle de Courtivron, eds, *New French Feminisms: An Anthology* (Amherst, Mass., 1980), p.xi.

57. Badia, *Féministe sans frontières*, p.9.

58. A recent study places the dividing line within the socialist women's movement itself; see Julie Carlier, *Moving Beyond Boundaries: An entangled history of feminism in Belgium, 1890-1914*, (Ghent; Univer siteit Gent, 2010).

59. Puschnerat asserts that 'the revolution became a religious duty for the marxist Zetkin', adding that she submitted to party discipline as early as 1921 and maintained it for the rest of her life, serving in 1925 as official prosecutor of the Social Revolutionary leaders in the trial that resulted in death sentences, later suspended. See Ünlüdag-Puschnerat 'Clara Zetkin: A German Communist', pp.100-106; and on suspension Vladimir Ilyich Lenin, 'The Comintern Executive following the confer ence of the three internationals', *Collected Works*, vol.42 (Moscow

1971), pp.415-416, n. 1. Toni Sender, socialist member of the Weimar Reichstag, reports that initially, at Berne, Zetkin resisted Leninist efforts to force party splits; Toni Sender, *The Autobiography of a German Rebel* (London, 1940), pp.63-64. Rappoport recalled her confiding in him in 1927 or 1928 that she detested Stalin; Rappoport, *Un Vie révolutionnaire*, p.108.

60. John S Partington reports on the esteem in which Zetkin continues to be held, 'On the Trail of Clara Zetkin', *Counterfire*, 16 April 2010, http://www.counterfire.org/index.php/features/75-our-history/4654-on-the-trail-of-clara-zetkin (accessed 30 July 2011).

61. Rappoport, *Une Vie révolutionnaire*, p.471; Louis Aragon, *The Bells of Basel*, tr. Haakon M Chevalier (New York, 1936), p.348 (originally published as *Les Cloches de Bâle*, 1934). For quotations from Zetkin's Basle speech, see Effi Böhlke, 'Clara Zetkin (1857-1933) und die internationale Solidarität', Studie, November-Dezember 2009 im Auftrag der Rosa-Luxemburg-Stiftung, [p.11].

62. On the First International, see my 'Foyer or Factory: Working Class Women in 19th Century France', in *Proceedings of the Second Annual Meeting, Western Society for French History*, ed. Brison D Gooch (College Station, Texas, 1975), pp.193-203.

63. *L'Equité*, 15 March 1914.

64. Zetkin to Jezierska, undated letter [probably about 1924] marked 15, Fanny Jezierska papers, Hoover Institution, Stanford University.

Chapter Two

1. This essay, which originated as a presentation to the conference of the International Federation for Research in Women's History during the 21st International Congress of Historical Sciences in Amsterdam in August 2010, constitutes my second exploration into Zetkin's relationship with the British socialist movement. For an earlier investigation, see John S Partington, 'Clara Zetkin's Reception in British Socialism and the British Women's Movement, 1889-1909', in *Anglosachsen: Leipzig und die englischsprachige Kultur*, ed. Stefan Welz and Fabian Dellemann (Frankfurt, 2010), pp.117-137. For my adventures in Germany, gathering information on Zetkin in Wiederau, Leipzig, Stuttgart and Birkenwerder, see Partington, 'On the Trail of Clara Zetkin', *Counterfire*, 16 April 2010, http://www.counterfire.org/ index.php/articles/75-our-history/4654-on-the-trail-of-clara-zetkin.

2. The newspapers I will focus on are as follows: the *Daily Herald* (retitled *The Herald* during the First World War as a weekly), the Labour Party newspaper; *Justice*, weekly journal of the Social Democratic

Federation (the Social Democratic Party from 1908 and the British Socialist Party from 1911); *Labour Leader*, the weekly of the Independent Labour Party; *The Clarion*, a non-partisan moderate socialist and labour weekly; and the *League Leaflet* (retitled *Labour Woman* in 1913) the monthly of the Women's Labour League.

3. Such perceived betrayals included opposition to the revolution in Russia in November 1917 and the crushing of the 1918-1919 revolution by the German social democratic government (including the murders of Karl Liebknecht and Rosa Luxemburg), not to mention support for the First World War by the majority of social democrats in most European countries.

4. The First Boer War had occurred in 1880-1881, when Boer farmers successfully rebelled against British rule in the Transvaal.

5. Clara Zetkin, 'May Greetings from Stuttgart', *Justice*, 12 May 1900 p.6.

6. For British socialist attitudes towards imperialism at this time, see Graham Johnson, *Social Democratic Politics in Britain 1881-191.* (Lewiston, 2002), pp.69-103. It was H M Hyndman, leader of the SDF who produced the anti-imperialist report for the 1904 Congress of the Second International. See Hyndman, *Colonies and Dependencies: Re port to the international socialist congress, held at Amsterdam, August 14th-20th, 1904* (London, 1904).

7. Zetkin uses this expression in the following English-language articles during the course of her career: Zetkin, 'May Greetings from Stuttgart' p.6; Zetkin, 'To the Socialist Women of All Countries', *Daily Herald*, 19 November 1912, p.2; Zetkin, 'Socialist Women & War. Protest by International Organisation', *Labour Leader*, 21 November 1912, p.756 Zetkin, 'War against War: To the Socialist Women of all Countries', *The Clarion*, 22 November 1912, p.6; Mary Macpherson, 'International Notes', *League Leaflet*, 24 (December 1912), p.8; Zetkin, 'Make Way for Peace! An Appeal from Klara Zetkin to the Women of Germany and of other Lands', *Labour Woman*, 2.9 (January 1915), p.268; and Zetkin, 'The International Communist Women's Day 1929', *International Press Correspondence*, 9.11 (1 March 1929), pp.183-184.

8. The ISB was the executive committee of the Second International.

9. See Zetkin, 'To the Socialist Women of All Countries', p.2; Zetkin 'Socialist Women & War', p.756; Zetkin, 'War against War', p.6; 'War against War – International Congress', *Justice*, 23 November 1912, p.6 and Macpherson, 'International Notes', p.8.

10. Zetkin, 'To the Socialist Women of All Countries', p.2.

11. Ibid., p.2.

12. Ibid., p.2.

13. Dora B Montefiore, *From a Victorian to a Modern* (London, 1927), rpt. *Marxist Internet Archive*, http://www.marxists.org/archive/monte fiore/1925/autobiography/12.htm (accessed 30 July 2011).

14. J. Keir Hardie, 'No European War! The International Socialist Congress', *Labour Leader*, 5 December 1912, p.783; Mary Macpherson, 'International Notes', *League Leaflet*, 25 (January 1913), p.12. Zetkin's representation of socialist women and her congress speech were also noted in 'Women's International Council of Socialist and Labour Organisations (British Section)', *League Leaflet*, 26 (February 1913), p.4; and Women's International Council of Socialist and Labour Organisations 'British Section)', in *Women's Labour League. Annual Report for the Year 1912, together with Report of Proceedings at the Eighth Annual Conference held in London, Tuesday, January 27th, 1913* (London, [1913]), pp.15-16.

15. 'Socialist Women and the International Demonstration at Basel', p.6.

16. Zetkin quoted in ibid., p.6.

17. Zetkin quoted in ibid, p.6. The closing quotation is from Thucydides, who reported that Spartan women would utter these words when presenting their menfolk with their shields ahead of battle, meaning that true Spartans could only return home either victorious or dead.

18. 'Und setzet ihr nicht das Leben ein / Nie wird euch das Leben gewonnen sein!' Zetkin quoting Schiller's 1799 drama, *Wallensteins Lager*, in 'Socialist Women and the International Demonstration at Basel', p.6. The report includes both the English and the German versions.

19. Mary Longman, 'Women's International Council of Socialist and Labour Organisations', *Labour Woman*, 1.7 (November 1913), p.106.

20. This visit was 'postponed, but may be undertaken before the Socialist Women's Congress at Vienna in August [1914]'. As the August congress was cancelled due to the outbreak of the First World War, one can assume the visit to Germany never took place. However, the same publication mentions that Mary Longman 'will shortly be visiting Germany and will therefore be able to meet the Committee which is making arrangements for the International Socialist Women's Conference'. See International Work', in *Women's Labour League. Annual Report for the Year 1913, together with Report of Proceedings at the Ninth Annual Conference held in Glasgow, Monday, January 26th, 1914* (London, 1914]), pp.14-15.

21. See Mary Longman, 'Women's International Council of Socialist and Labour Organisations', *Labour Woman*, 1.8 (December 1913), p.119.

22. Zetkin, 'German Women to their Sisters in Great Britain', *Th* *Labour Woman*, 1.8 (December 1913), p.111.

23. Ibid., p.111; emphasis in the original.

24. Ibid., p.111.

25. Ibid., p.111.

26. Ibid., p.111.

27. 'The *Gleichheit* Suppressed', *Justice*, 17 December 1914, p.1.

28. The British attendees were delegated by the following organisations Women's Labour League (Longman); Women's International Counci (Phillips); the ILP and Women's Trade Union League (Bondfield) and th ILP (Salter). See 'Women's War against War: Towards the New Socialis International', *Labour Woman*, 2.12 (April 1915), p.285; and 'Bravo Our Women! International Conference Held', *Labour Leader*, 8 Apri 1915, p.7.

29. Mary Longman, 'Our Sisters Abroad', *Labour Woman*, 2.11 (Marcl 1915), p.282.

30. Longman, 'Our Sisters Abroad', p.282.

31. 'Women's War against War', pp.285-86.

32. Ibid., p.285.

33. Ibid., p.285.

34. Ibid., p.286.

35. The countries represented were Britain, Germany, France, Russia Poland, the Netherlands, Switzerland and Italy.

36. 'Bravo, Our Women!', p.7. For endorsing compensation to Belgiun at the conclusion of the war, the American socialist, William Englisl Walling, wrote of Zetkin that she 'is [the SPD's] only member who ha been put on record as favoring any peace terms which Socialist pacifist outside of Germany would consider as a real concession'. See Williar English Walling, ed., *The Socialists and the War: A documentary state ment of the position of the socialists of all countries; with special refe ence to their peace policy, including a summary of the revolutionary stat socialist measures adopted by the governments at war* (New York, 1915) p.442.

37. 'Bravo, Our Women!', p.7.

38. 'Women and Peace', *The Herald*, 10 April 1915, p.2.

39. 'The Socialist Women's International: Inspiring manifesto', *Labou Leader*, 22 April 1915, p.3.

40. Ibid., p.3.

41. Ibid., p.3.

42. Marion Phillips, 'The Women's International: A May message to the working women of all lands. Report of the extraordinary conference of labour and socialist women held at Berne, Switzerland, on March 27th, 28th and 29th, 1915', *Labour Woman*, 3.1 (May 1915), p.291. The conference dates were actually 26-28 March.

43. Marion Phillips, 'The Women's International', *Contemporary Review*, 593 (May 1915), pp.646-651.

44. Phillips, 'The Women's International: A May message...', p.293.

45. Ibid., p.293.

46. Ibid.,p.293.

47. Ibid., p.293.

48. Phillips's account of the Russian delegation is unclear in regard to numbers and political affiliation. She states, 'The Russian delegation consisted of two groups consisting altogether of seven. Poland sent one representative [...]. The important Organising Committee of the Social Democratic Labour Party was however represented by two of the Russians'. The implication here is that seven Russian and a Pole attended the conference. However, Olga Ravich claims 'Russia was represented by two delegations: that of the Central Committee, which consisted of five persons – Sablina (Nadezhda Konstantinovna), Inessa, Elena Rozmirovich), Zina (Lilina), and Anna [Kaminskaia] (representative of Poland) – and that of the Menshevik Organization Committee, which consisted of two persons, Balabanoff and Irina Izolskaia'. Here, the Russian delegation of seven *includes* the Pole. While Ravich's account seems more detailed than Phillips's, she was writing ten years after the conference, and it is unclear whether she herself attended. Phillips, on the other hand was a delegate, and published her account shortly after the event. See Phillips, 'The Women's International: A May Message...', p.293; and Olga Ravich, 'Unofficial Account of the International Conference of Socialist Women at Berne, March 26-28, 1915', in *The Bolsheviks and the World War: The origin of the Third International*, by Olga Hess Gankin and H H Fisher (Stanford, 1960), pp.288-95 (p.289).

49. Phillips, 'The Women's International: A May message...', p.293.

50. Ibid., p.294.

51. Ibid., p.294.

52. Ibid., p.293.

53. Ibid., p.295.

54. The International Conference of Socialist and Labour Women, Manifesto to the Working Women of Belligerent Countries from the

International Conference of Socialist and Labour Women', *Labour Woman*, 3.2 (June 1915), p.303.

55. Ibid., p.303.

56. In April 1917 *Labour Woman* reported receipt of 'a message from our International Socialist Secretary, Clara Zetkin', suggesting an International Socialist and Labour Women's Conference immediately at the close of the war. See 'Women After the War', *Labour Woman*, 4.12 (April 1917), p.137. In the August 1917 issue of the same journal, Cedar Paul, the secretary of the British branch of the SWI, reports a letter received from Zetkin (via Heleen Ankersmit) 'referring to the possibility of an international congress of socialist women to discuss questions of reconstruction'. See Cedar Paul, 'Women's International Council', *Labour Woman*, 5.4 (August 1917), p.191. In the event, neither conference took place.

57. Between 1917 and 1919 Zetkin was a member of the Independent Social Democratic Party, as well as active in the Spartacist Group.

58. Clara Zetkin, 'Clara Zetkin (*Editor of the German Socialist Women's Paper*)', in 'German Socialists Want Peace. Official Message to the *Labour Leader*. Greetings from Dr Liebknecht and Rosa Luxemburg', *Labour Leader*, 31 December 1914, pp.1-2. Zetkin again prophesied the coming of a 'third international' in 1916, when she wrote of socialist women: 'They know that the Berne Conference will bear fruit in the days to come. A time will come – perhaps sooner than we think – when the workers in their multitudes will write across the streams of blood in a third International'. See Zetkin, 'The Women's International: A message for women's day in Holland from Clara Zetkin (international secretary)', *Labour Woman*, 4.1 (May 1916), p.5.

59. Zetkin, 'The International Communist Women's Day 1929', p.183.

60. Zetkin, *The Toilers Against War* (London, 1934).

Chapter Three

1. See, for example, N Chegina's letter to Clara Zetkin, requesting her agreement to name a nursery after her in the village Kuzovino, Tver region (date unknown), typed transcript, Clara Zetkin Fond, Russian State Archive of Social and Political History, Moscow (hereafter abbreviated as RGASPI), 528/1/1702; Clara Zetkin's letter to the commander and crew of the steamship 'Klara Tsetkin', 13 June 1931, typed transcript, Clara Zetkin Fond, RGASPI, 528/1/180; Clara Zetkin's letter to the personnel of the third tobacco factory named after 'Klara Tsetkin' 27 March 1932, typed transcript, Clara Zetkin Fond, RGASPI

28/1/190; N. Nashivochnikov, ed., *Klara Tsetkin zovet k mezhdunarodnoi solidarnosti* (Moscow, 1934), p.23.

2. See, for example, Zetkin, *Zhenskiy vopros i germanskoe studenchestvo* (The woman question and German studenthood) (Odessa, 1905); Zetkin, *Zhenshchina i ee ekonomicheskoe polozhenie* (Woman and her economic condition) (Odessa, 1905); Zetkin, *Intelligentnyy proletariat, zhenskiy vopros i sotsializm* (The educated proletariat, the woman question and socialism) (Odessa, 1905); Zetkin, *Nachalo zhenskogo rabochego dvizheniya v Germanii* (Beginnings of the working women's movement in Germany) (St. Petersburg, 1906); Zetkin, *Shkol'nyi vopros i rabochiy klass* (The school question and the working class) (Moscow, 1917); Zetkin, *Za bol'shevikov!* (In support of Bolsheviks!) (Moscow, 1918); Zetkin, *Bor'ba za svobodu i mir v Rossii* (The struggle for freedom and peace in Russia) (Moscow, 1919); Zetkin, *Bortsy revolutsii* (Fighters for revolution) (Petrograd, 1920); Zetkin, *Karl Marx i delo ego zhizni* (Karl Marx and his life work) (Moscow, 1922); Zetkin, *Roza Lyuksemburg i russkaya revolyutsiya* (Rosa Luxemburg and the Russian revolution) (Moscow, 1923); Zetkin, *Kavkaz v ogne* (The Caucasus ablaze) (Moscow, 1926); etc.

3. *Tsetkin: sbornik statei i materialov* (Moscow, 1933), p.10.

4. See, for example, Zinaida Boyarskaya, *Tsetkin*, 2nd edn (Moscow and Leningrad, 1928), pp.7-8 (originally published, 1926); Galina Serebryakova, *Pod Krasnoy Zvezdoy. Klara Tsetkin* (Moscow, 1967), p.35.

6. Avgust Bebel', *Zhenshchina i sotsializm* (*Woman and Socialism*) (Petrograd, 1918). The majority of socialists politically active and influential at the time of the Russian revolutions represented the younger generation of the 1870s. To name but a few, Lenin was born in 1870, his wife Krupskaya in 1869, Kollontai in 1872 and Elena Stasova in 1873.

7. Kollontai, 'Avtobiografiya seksual'no emansipirovannoy komunistki' (*The Autobiography of a Sexually Emancipated Communist Woman*), in *Marksistskiy feminizm. Kollektsiya tekstov A. M. Kollontai* (Tver, 2003), p.10. See also Wendy Goldman, *Women, the State and Revolution: Soviet family policy and social life, 1917-1936* (Cambridge, 1993), p.43.

8. Kollontai papers, RGASPI, 134/1/88/10.

9. Kollontai, 'Zhenskoe rabochee dvizhenie' (Women's labour movement), in *Marksistskiy feminizm. Kollektsiya tekstov A. M. Kollontai* (Tver, 2003), p.101.

10. Angelica Balabanova, *Moya zhizn' – bor'ba. Memuary russkoy sotsialistki, 1897-1938*, (*My Life as a Rebel*) (Moscow, 2007), p.29; Nadezhda Krupskaya, *Klara Tsetkin* (Moscow, 1933), pp.12-13.

11. Before that, Kollontai, a devoted Marxist activist, travelled a lc around Europe and had time to make personal connections with som eminent socialist figures; Roṣa Luxemburg, Karl Kautsky, Paul an Laura Lafargue were among them.

12. Zetkin to Kollontai, 21 March 1909, typed transcript, Clara Zetkir Fond, RGASPI, 528/1/200. See also Kollontai, *Izbrannye stat'i i recl* (Selected articles and speeches) (Moscow, 1972), p.415.

13. Kollontai reported about the SWI conferences in a pamphlet 'Mezhdunarodnye sotsialisticheskie soveshaniya rabotnits (International socialist conferences of women workers), first publishec in Russian in 1918. She witnessed that during the women's conferenc at Stuttgart in 1907, German women suggested creating an Interna tional Women's Secretariat to gather and analyse information abour women's movements. In the end, there was a resolution to consider *Di Gleichheit* editorial staff the central bureau of the SWI (Kollontai *Izbrannye stat'i i rechi*, pp.92-94).

14. Kollontai refers in her autobiography to the fact that she attendec the Fourth German Socialist Women's Conference in Mannheim on 22-23 September 1906. See Aleksandra Kollontai, *Izbrannye stat'i rechi*, p.99, n.34.

15. Kollontai, 'Dva techeniya (po povodu pervoy mezhdunarodnoy zhenskoy konferentsii v Shtutgarte)' (Two trends [regarding the first international women's conference in Stuttgart]), *Obrazovanie*, 16 (October 1907), pp.46-62; Kollontai, 'Zhenshchina-rabotnitsa v sovre- mennom obshchestve' (Woman worker in modern society), in *Trudy Pervogo Vserossiyskogo zhenskogo s"ezda* (St Petersburg, 1908), pp.792-801.

16. Kollontai, *Sotsialnye osnovy zhenskogo voprosa* (The social basis of the woman question) (St Petersburg, 1909).

17. See Zetkin to Kollontai, 1909-1914, typed transcript, Clara Zetkin Fond, RGASPI, 528/1/198-245.

18. Lenin, *Polnoe sobranie sochineniy* (Complete Works), vol. 49 (Moscow, 1964), pp.138-139.

19. Kollontai, *Izbrannye stat'i i rechi*, pp.418-421.

20. Angelica Balabanoff, *Impressions of Lenin* (Ann Arbor, 1964), pp.40- 41.

21. Masao Nishikawa, *Socialists and International Actions for Peace, 1914-1923* (Berlin, 2010), p.37.

21. Kollontai, *Izbrannye stat'i i rechi*, p.419.

22. Cited in Richard Stites, *The Women's Liberation Movement in Russia: Feminism, nihilism, and Bolshevism, 1860-1930* (Princeton, 1991), p.285.

23. In fact, Farnsworth merely records her assumptions about the nature of the disagreement between Zetkin and Kollontai; as she puts it, 'Kollontai may have reminded Zetkin of old enemies' (namely Lily Braun). Her more solid argument refers to the debates in the International Women's Secretariat, and in this part of her reasoning she follows E H Carr's outline of the history of the Third International. Beatrice Farnsworth, *Alexandra Kollontai: Socialism, feminism, and the Bolshevik revolution* (Stanford, 1980), pp.260-267; E H Carr, *Socialism in One Country, 1924-1926*, vol.3, part II (London, 1964), pp.976-987.

24. It appears that Zetkin wrote her last business letter to Kollontai in February 1921 (Zetkin to Kollontai, 1 February 1921, typed transcript, Clara Zetkin Fond, RGASPI, 528/1/246); later, in her writings, Zetkin did not even mention Kollontai. The latter, from her side, did not criticise Zetkin publicly and did not declare that she was disappointed with her (as Angelica Balabanova did in her memoir, *Moya zhizn' – bor'ba...*, p.304). Kollontai even made an attempt to restore contact; she wrote a letter to Zetkin in March 1933 where she congratulated Zetkin on being rewarded with the Lenin Order, shared her recollections of their cooperation in the past and expressed her admiration for the courage Zetkin had displayed during the opening of the Reichstag (Kollontai to Zetkin, 14 March 1933, Clara Zetkin Fond, RGASPI, 528/1/1091). I have found no evidence that Clara Zetkin answered this letter.

25. Zinaida Boyarskaya, *Klara Tsetkin* (Moscow and Leningrad, 1928), p.32.

26. Nadezhda Krupskaya, *Klara Tsetkin*, p.17.

27. There is some indirect evidence in support of this statement. See, for example, a letter written by a Moscow orphanage's pupils to Clara Zetkin to support her and protest against the German government's order to arrest her, 30 March 1924, typed transcript, Clara Zetkin Fond, RGASPI, 528/2/316; see also a hostile letter written to Zetkin by students of the University of Berlin, 30 August 1932, typed transcript, Clara Zetkin Fond, RGASPI, 528/2/411.

28. About Zetkin's relations with soviet leaders, see Luise Dornemann, *Clara Zetkin: Ein Lebensbild* (Berlin, 1962; Russian edition, 1976); Gilbert Badia, *Clara Zetkin: Eine neue Biographie* (Berlin, 1994); and Tânia Puschnerat, *Clara Zetkin: Bürgerlichkeit und marxismus* (Essen, 2003).

29. Elena Stasova, *Klara Tsetkin* (Omsk, 1937), p.2. For the erroneou later date, see Olga Runova, *Babushka kommunizma Klara Tsetki* (Moscow, 1924), p.25; Nadezhda Krupskaya, *Klara Tsetkin*, p.19; an Klara Tsetkin: sbornik statei i materialov, p.8.

30. Zetkin to Krupskaya, 27 March 1920, typed transcript, Clara Zetki Fond, RGASPI, 528/1/311.

31. Cited in Olga Runova, *Babushka kommunizma Klara Tsetkin*, p.25

32. Angelica Balabanova, *Moya zhizn' – bor'ba*, p.302.

33. Zetkin to Krupskaya, 10 February 1932, typed transcript, Clara Zetkin Fond, RGASPI, 528/1/308.

34. Angelica Balabanova, *Moya zhizn' – bor'ba*, p.303.

35. For 'Bolshevizing', see Tânia Puschnerat, *Clara Zetkin*, p.235.

36. Zetkin reported on 'agitation work' in the following letters: Clara Zetkin to O V Kuusinen, 4 October 1924, typed transcript, Clara Zetkir Fond, RGASPI, 528/2/151; Clara Zetkin to Maxim Zetkin, 9 Augus 1925, typed transcript, Clara Zetkin Fond, RGASPI, 528/2/218. Abou Zetkin's plans to go to Central Asia, see Clara Zetkin to the Centra Committee of the Communist Party of Uzbekistan, 3 March 1927, typec transcript, Clara Zetkin Fond, RGASPI, 528/1/687.

37. Zetkin, *Kavkaz v ogne*, translated by S. Sheverdin (Moscow, Leningrad, 1926); Zetkin, 'Was die Frauen Lenin verdanken', *Die Kommunistische Fraueninternationale* 5.1 (January 1925), pp.1-12.

38. RGASPI, 528/2/439.

39. The patronymic of Lenin – Il'ich – had been widely used singly in spoken language and writings to emphasise accessibility and closeness, a kinship between Lenin and the common people.

40. Clara Zetkin, *Vospominaniya o Lenine* (Moscow, 1966), pp.3-4. The first edition of the book is Zetkin, *O Lenine. Vospominaniya i vstrechi*. Translated from manuscript, edited by S. Sheverdin (Moscow, 1924). Later, the book was reprinted six times; the last edition appearing in 1976. It appears in English as *Reminiscences of Lenin* (New York, 1929).

41. Clara Zetkin to Konstantin Zetkin, 13 March 1928, typed transcript, Clara Zetkin Fond, RGASPI, 528/1/712.

42. On Zetkin's membership in the All-Union Society for Old Bolsheviks, see RGASPI, 528/1/871 and 528/1/1769.

43. Zetkin to Elena Stasova, 27 February 1924, typed transcript, Clara Zetkin Fond, RGASPI, 528/1/543. See also Zetkin to Stasova, 8 April 1924, RGASPI, 528/1/555, 528/1/556; Zetkin to (Karl), 27 February 1924, autograph, RGASPI, 528/2/191; Zetkin to Elena Stasova, 14

January 1925, typed transcript, RGASPI, 528/2/456; Zetkin to Konstantin Zetkin, 16 March 1928, RGASPI, 528/1/713.

44. Zetkin to Krupskaya, Maria Ulyanova and Anna Ulyanova, 15 March 1931, typed transcript, Clara Zetkin Fond, RGASPI, 528/1/307.

45. Olga Runova, *Babushka kommunizma Klara Tsetkin* (Moscow, 1924); *Klara Tsetkin: sbornik statei i materialov* (Moscow, 1933), pp.6, 9.

46. *Clara Tsetkin zovet k mezhdunarodnoy solidarnosti*, p.23.

47. Nadezhda Krupskaya, *Klara Tsetkin*, p.20.

Chapter Four

1. This chapter draws on the following publications by the author: Florence Hervé, ed., *Clara Zetkin oder: Dort kämpfen, wo das Leben ist* (Clara Zetkin or: to fight there where life is), 3rd edn (Berlin, 2011); Florence Hervé, 'In Frankreich geschätzt, in der Bundesrepublik diffamiert? Erfahrungen mit der Rezeption von Clara Zetkin' (Appreciated in France, slandered in the Federal Republic of Germany? Some experiences about the reception of Clara Zetkin), in *'Ich kann nicht gegen meine Überzeugung handeln'. Clara Zetkin zum 150. Geburtstag*, ed. Astrid Franzke and Ilse Nagelschmidt (Leipzig, 2008), pp.103-116, and Florence Hervé, 'Vilipendée à l'ouest, encensée à l'est? Autour de la réception de Clara Zetkin à l'occasion de son 150e anniversaire' (Run down in the West, glorified in the East? On Clara Zetkin's reception on the occasion of her 150th birthday), *Allemagne d'aujourd'hui*, 181 (July-September 2007), pp.148-152.

2. Cited in Gilbert Badia, *Clara Zetkin: Féministe sans frontières* (Clara Zetkin: Feminist without frontiers) (Paris, 1993). The German edition is *Clara Zetkin. Eine neue Biographie* (Clara Zetkin: A new biography), trans. F. Hervé and I. Nödinger (Berlin, 1994). Until 1933 there was a distinction between the bourgeois women's movement which emerged out of the revolution of 1848 under the leadership of Louise Otto-Peters, and the proletarian women's movement which, in the late nineteenth and the early twentieth century, under the leadership of Clara Zetkin, was bound to the trade union organisation of working women and to the development of a Marxist theory of emancipation. The main revendications of the former were votes for women and the rights to work and to education, and it sought reforms within capitalist society. The latter was revolutionary and aimed at the emancipation of women within a socialist society.

3. Alice Schwarzer, *Der kleine Unterschied und seine großen Folgen* (The small difference and its big impact) (Cologne, 1975), p.238.

4. Marielouise Janssen-Jurreit: *Sexismus. Über die Abtreibung de Frauenfrage* (Sexism: On the miscarriage of the woman question (Munich, 1976), p.229.

5. Clara Zetkin, *Zur Geschichte der proletarischen Frauenbewegung i Deutschland* (On the history of the proletarian women's movement i Germany) (Frankfurt, 1979); Karin Bauer, *Clara Zetkin und die proletai ische Frauenbewegung* (Clara Zetkin and the proletarian women' movement) (Berlin, 1978). 'Karin Bauer' is the pseudonym for Antj Vollmer, former representative of the Green Party in the Bundestag. Se also Pascal Beucker, 'Mythen in Tüten' (Some legends), *Konkret*, (1996), pp.21-23.

6. Zetkin, *Zur Geschichte der proletarischen Frauenbewegung Deutsch lands* (On the history of the proletarian women's movement in Germa ny) (Frankfurt, 1978); Zetkin, *Für die Sowjemacht* (For the power of th soviets) (Frankfurt, 1977); and Gisela Elsner, 'Clara Zetkin', in *Frauen Porträts aus zwei Jahrhunderten*, ed. Hans Jürgen Schultz (Stuttgart 1981), pp.158-171.

7. 'Clara Zetkin', ed. Abt. Frauenpolitik beim DKP-Parteivorstanc (Düsseldorf, 1987).

8. Photocopy of the document. Archives of the author.

9. Gisela Kessler to the author, quoted in Florence Hervé, 'In Frankreich geschätzt, in der Bundesrepublik diffamiert?', p.112.

10. Friedhelm Boll, 'Clara Zetkin und die proletarische Frauenbewe gung. Sozialismus als Familienschicksal' (Clara Zetkin and the prole tarian women's movement. Socialism as family destiny), in *Die geteilte Utopie. Sozialisten in Frankreich und in Deutschland*, ed. Marieluise Christadler (Opladen, 1985), p.66ff.

11. Joan Reutershan, *Clara Zetkin und Brot und Rosen* (Clara Zetkin and bread and roses) (New York, 1985).

12. Luise Dornemann, *Clara Zetkin. Leben und Wirken* (Clara Zetkin. Life and action) (Berlin, 1957 / 1974), pp.5-9.

13. Ibid., pp.499-549.

14. Lilo Hardel, *Das Mädchen aus Wiederau* (The girl from Wiederau) (Berlin, 1964).

15. The following works by Zetkin were published in the GDR: *Aus gewählte Reden und Schriften* (Selected speeches and writings), 3 vols (Berlin, 1957-1960); *Zur Geschichte der proletarischen Frauenbewegung Deutschlands* (Berlin, 1958); *Kunst und Proletariat* (Art and the proletar iat) (Berlin, 1977); *Zur Theorie und Taktik der kommunistischen Bewe gung* (On the theory and practice of the communist movement), ed. Katja Haferkorn and Heinz Karl (Leipzig, 1974); *Für die Sowjetmacht*.

Artikel, Reden und Briefe 1917-1933 (For the power of the soviets. Articles, speeches and letters 1917-1933) (Berlin, 1977); and *Erinnerungen an Lenin. Mit einem Anhang: Aus dem Briefwechsel Clara Zetkins mit W.I. Lenin und N.K. Krupskaja* (Reminiscences of Lenin. With Appendix: Letters between Clara Zetkin, V.I. Lenin and N.K. Krupskaya) (Berlin, 1955).

16. These museums still exist: Clara-Zetkin-Gedenkstätte Wiederau, Museum Alte Dorfschule, 09306 Königshain-Wiederau, and Clara-Zetkin-Gedenkstätte Birkenwerder, Summter Straße 4, 16547 Birkenwerder, respectively.

17. Zetkin, *Zur Theorie und Taktik der kommunistischen Bewegung*.

18. Zetkin, *Clara Zetkin über Jugenderziehung* (Clara Zetkin on youth education) (Berlin, 1957); Rosemarie Walther, *Clara Zetkin zur proletarischen Familienerziehung* (Clara Zetkin on proletarian family education) (Berlin, 1959); Gerd Hohendorf, *Revolutionäre Schulpolitik und marxistische Pädagogik im Lebenswerk Clara Zetkins* (Revolutionary school policy and Marxist pedagogy in Clara Zetkin's lifework) (Berlin, 1962); and Clara Zetkin, *Revolutionäre Bildungspolitik und marxistische Pädagogik: Ausgewählte Reden und Schriften* (Revolutionary education policy and Marxist pedagogy: Selected speeches and writings) (Berlin, 1983).

19. Zetkin, *Über Literatur und Kunst* (On literature and art), ed. Emilia Milowidowa (Berlin, 1955); and Clara Zetkin, *Kunst und Proletariat* (Berlin, 1977).

20. Hans-Jürgen Arendt, 'Forschungen zu Leben und Werk Clara Zetkins in der DDR' (Research on Clara Zetkin's life and work in the GDR), in *'Ich kann nicht gegen meine Überzeugung handeln'*, p.90.

21. Hans-Jürgen Arendt, 'Forschungen zu Leben und Werk Clara Zetkins in der DDR', paper presented at the conference, 'Die Frauenpolitikerin Clara Zetkin – zum 150. Geburtstag', University of Leipzig, 26-27 June 2007.

22. Correspondence between Badia and several publishing houses, September to October 1993. See Gilbert Badia, *Clara Zetkin: Féministe sans frontières*; Gilbert Badia, *Clara Zetkin. Eine neue Biographie*.

23. In France, *La Pensée* (April 1993), pp.136-138; *Témoignage Aco*, 404 (June 1993); *Politis* (1993) pp.127-128; *Le Monde libertaire*, *La Lettre de l'EDM* (1993); *L'OURS* (April 1993) pp.9-10; *Révolution* (18 March 1993) pp.38-40; and *Clara-Magazine*, 93 (Spring 1993), pp.2-3. In Germany, *Die Zeit*, 36 (2 September 1994), literary pages; *Südwestfunk S2 Kultur* (4 November 1994), manuscript of the radio broadcast; *ekz-Informationsdienst*, 30 (1994); *Z-Marxistische Erneuerung* (December 1994), pp.235-241; *M-zeitschrift der IG-Medien* (March

1995), p.36; *Leipzigs Neue*, 21 (21 October 1994); *Zeitschrift für Geschichtswissenschaften* (January 1994), p.71; *Rote Fahne* (5 November 1994); *Neues Deutschland* (21 March 1994), p.10; *Esprit* (October 1994), p.17; *Ariadne-Almanach des Archivs der deutschen Frauenbewegung*, 26 (November 1994), p.72; 'Was Frau liest' (What women read), *DGB-Frauenoffensive* (April 1994); *wir frauen*, 1 (Frühjahr 1994), pp.22-23; and *Frauen in der Geschichte, zeitzschrift des Vereins*, 1 (1994), pp.137-141.

24. *Die Zeit*, 36 (2 September 1994), literary pages.

25. Tânia Puschnerat, *Clara Zetkin, Bürgerlichkeit und Marxismus* (Clara Zetkin, bourgeois manners and Marxism) (Essen, 2003), p.413

26. Marieluise Christadler in *metis*, 1 (1994), pp.123-125; archives Gilbert Badia, letter from Friedhelm Boll to Gilbert Badia, 4 November 1993.

27. Lila Offensive, ed., *Dokumentation der Proteste gegen die geplante Umbenennung der Clara-Zetkin-Straße* (Documents on the protests against changing the name of Clara-Zetkin-Straâe) (Berlin, 1994).

28. Cited in ibid.

29. Interview with Gilbert Badia, cited in 'In würdiger antifaschistischer Tradition' (In a deserving anti-fascist tradition), *Freitag* (7 June 1994).

30. The speech was published in Germany in *Marxistische Blätter*, 3 (1995), pp.17-29, and in France in *Batailles pour les femmes*, ed. Gilbert Badia, et al. (Paris, 1980), pp.139-163.

31. Tânia Puschnerat, *Clara Zetkin, Bürgerlichkeit und Marxismus* (Essen, 2003). See also the review of the book by Gilbert Badia and Florence Hervé, 'Zetkin revidiert. Einige Bemerkungen zur Biografie von Tânia Puschnerat über Clara Zetkin' (Zetkin revised. Some remarks on Tânia Puschnerat's biography of Clara Zetkin), *junge Welt*, 7/8 (August 2004), Wochenendbeilage, p.6.

32. Gisela Greulich-Janssen, 'Clara Zetkin – Kämpferin für die Rechte der Frauen' (Clara Zetkin – a fighter for women's rights), in *Das Ideal der Mitmenschlichkeit. Frauen und die sozialistische Idee*, ed. Elke Pilz (Würzburg, 2005), pp.9-29; and Irma Hildebrand, 'Die Politikerin Clara Zetkin' (The politician Clara Zetkin), in *Mutige Frauen. 30 Porträts aus fünf Jahrhunderten* (Munich, 2005), pp.185-199.

33. Florence Hervé, ed., *Clara Zetkin oder: Dort kämpfen, wo das Leben ist*; Astrid Franzke and Ilse Nagelschmidt, eds, *'Ich kann nicht gegen meine Überzeugung handeln'. Clara Zetkin zum 150. Geburtstag* ('I cannot act against my convictions', Clara Zetkin on the occasion of her 150th birthday) (Leipzig, 2008); Ulla Plener, ed., *Clara Zetkin in ihrer Zeit. Neue Fakten, Erkenntnisse, Wertungen. Material des Kolloquiums*

nlässlich ihres 150. Geburtstages am 6. Juli 2007 in Berlin (Clara
etkin in her time. New facts, knowledge and appreciations. Materials
·om the colloquium on the occasion of her 150th birthday on 6 July
·007 in Berlin) (Berlin, 2008). Radio features included: "'Als seien mir
lügel gewachsen". Das Leben der Clara Zetkin. Zum 150. Geburtstag
·er Frauenrechtlerin' ('As if I had grown wings'. The life of Clara Zetkin.
·n the occasion of the 150th birthday of the women's fighter), 4 July
·007, 22.00-23.00, MDR FIGARO; and '5. Juli 1857: Geburtstag der
·olitikerin Clara Zetkin' (5 July 1857. Anniversary of the politician
·lara Zetkin), 5 July 2007, 09:05, WDR 5, ZEITZEICHEN.

·4. 100 Jahre Waldheim Stuttgart e.V. Clara-Zetkin-Haus (100 years of
·e Waldheim Stuttgart e.V. Clara-Zetkin-Haus) (Stuttgart, 2009).

·5. Florence Hervé, 'Zum 100. Jahrestag des Beschlusses von Kopen-
·agen zur Einführung des Internationalen Frauentags' (On the 100th
·nniversary of the decision in Copenhagen to introduce International
·Vomen's Day), 18. Louise-Otto-Peters-Tagung, Leipzig, 19-20 Novem-
·er 2010.

·6. Clara Zetkin, Zur Frage des Frauenwahlrechts (On the question of
·omen's votes) (Bremen, 2010).

·7. Ute Gerhard, Petra Pommerenke and Ulla Wischermann, eds,
·lassikerinnen feministischer Theorie. Grundlagentexte (Women's clas-
·ics of feminist theory. Basic texts), vol.1 (1789-1919); Ulla Wischer-
·nann, Susanne Rauscher and Ute Gerhard, eds, vol.2 (1920-1985)
·(önigstein and Taunus, 2008/2010); and Gudrun Ankele, ed., abso-
·ute Feminismus (absolute feminism) (Freiburg, 2010).

·8. Susanne Gretter, 'Clara Zetkin', FemBio, http://www.fembio.org/
·iographie.php/frau/biographie/clara-zetkin (accessed 31 July 2011).

Chapter Five

. I have dealt more fully with these questions in chapters 1 and 8 of
·usan Zimmermann, GrenzÜberschreitungen. Internationale Netzwerke,
·)rganisationen, Bewegungen und die Politik der globalen Ungleichheit
·om 17. bis zum 21. Jahrhundert (Vienna, 2010).

·. Susan Zimmermann, 'The challenge of multinational empire for the
·nternational women's movement: The case of the Habsburg Monarchy',
·n Globalizing Feminisms, 1789-1945, ed. Karen Offen (Abingdon and
·Jew York, 2010), pp.153-169, 367-373.

·. Susan Zimmermann, 'A struggle over gender, class and the vote:
·nequal international interaction and the birth of the "female Interna-
·ional" of socialist women (1905-1907)', in Gender History in a Transna-

tional Perspective, ed. Oliver Janz and Daniel Schönpflug (New York forthcoming).

4. V. Levinsky, *L'internationale socialiste et les peuples opprimé* (Vienna, 1920), pp.69-79; Michael Löwy, *Internationalismus und National alismus. Kritische Essays zu Marxismus und 'nationaler Frage'* (Köln 1999), pp.51-56; Georges Haupt, ed., *Bureau socialiste internationa Comptes rendus des réunions, manifestes et circulaires*, vol.1: 190C 1907 (Matériaux pour l'histoire du socialisme international, 1. Premiè série, textes et documents, II) (Paris, 1969), pp.106-107, 124. A translations from the German and the French throughout this essa are mine.

5. Zimmermann, 'Challenge', pp.158-162.

6. II. Internationale RY 4/ I 6/2/21 (sheets 16 ff.), Stiftung Archiv de Parteien und Massenorganisationen im Bundesarchiv (Berlin) (cited a SAPMO-BArch in the following); *Congrès socialiste international. Stut gart 6-24 août 1907*, VIII (Histoire de la IIe Internationale 16-18 Suppl (Geneva, 1978-1985), vol.16, pp.193-196; Haupt, *Bureau socialist international*, pp.251-254 (French version).

7. Zimmermann, *GrenzÜberschreitungen*, pp.161-165.

8. *Die Gleichheit*, 17 (1907), p.139.

9. Russia was not represented either among the official delegates *Congrès socialiste 1907*, vol.17, pp.303, 311.

10. *Congrès international socialiste des travailleurs et des chambre syndicales ouvrières. Londres 26 juillet – 2 août 1896*, V (Histoire de l IIe Internationale 10) (Geneva, 1980), pp.468-471; Maxim Anin, 'Da Nationalitätsprinzip in der Sozialistischen Internationale', *Sozialis tische Monatshefte*, 14.2 (1910), pp.885-890, 889; *Congrès socialist 1907*, vol.16, p.lv; Haupt, *Bureau socialiste international*, pp.280, 288

11. *Die Gleichheit*, 17 (1907), p.150; *Congrès socialiste 1907*, vol.17 pp.309, 311, 325.

12. See Haupt, *Bureau socialiste international*, p.209.

13. *Congrès international socialiste 1896*, p.152.

14. *Berichte an die Zweite Internationale Konferenz sozialistischer Frau en zu Kopenhagen am 26. und 27. August 1910* (Stuttgart, n. d.) pp.20-24.

15. In German the term 'Weiber', while in earlier centuries pointing t women in general and ordinary women in particular, by the early 20th century was used in either a derogatory or, as in this case, an ironi manner; in other words Rosa Luxemburg in her letter was making fur of the conference. Rosa Luxemburg, *Gesammelte Briefe*, 5 vols (Berlin

1982-1984), vol.3, pp.199, 223-225 (emphasis in the original). Galicia here refers to the Kingdom of Galicia and Lodomeria which formed part of Cisleithania.

16. *Vorwärts*, 28 August 1910, 3d supplement, pp.1-2; 30 August 1910, 3d supplement, p.1; *Congrès socialiste international. Copenhague 28 août – 3 septembre 1910*, IX (Histoire de la IIe Internationale 19-21) (Geneva, 1981-1982), vol.19, pp.906-910.

17. See for example *Die Gleichheit*, 22 (1911/1912), p.126.

18. *Die Gleichheit*, 21 (1910/1911), p.9; *Vorwärts*, 28 August 1910, 3d supplement, pp.1-2.

19. *Vorwärts*, 28 August 1910, 3d supplement, p.1.

20. The quote is from the Berne Resolution of 1915, II. Internationale RY 4/ I 6/2/69 (sheets 5-6), SAPMO-BArch (italics in the original); see also Nachlass Clara Zetkin NY 4005/35, SAPMO-BArch.

21. *Vorwärts*, 30 August 1910, 3d supplement, p.1.

22. *Die Gleichheit*, 17 (1907), p.150; *Vorwärts*, 28 August 1910, 3d supplement, p.1.

23. *Vorwärts*, 28 August 1910, 3d supplement.

24. This is Georges Haupt's wording in his introduction to *Congrès socialiste 1907*, vol.17, p.15.

25. G D H Cole, *The Second International, 1889-1914* (London, 1963), pp.62-70, 82-85; Georges Haupt, 'Einleitung', in *Congrès international extraordinaire. Bâle 24-25 Novembre 1912*, X (Histoire de la IIe Internationale, 22) (Genève, 1980), pp.11-14.

26. *Die Gleichheit*, 17 (1907), p.139.

27. *Congrès socialiste 1907*, vol.17, p.322.

28. *Die Gleichheit*, 18 (1908), p.80; 19 (1908/1909), pp.232-233.

29. So the wording went in the lead article on the 'international meetings at Copenhagen'. *Die Gleichheit*, 20 (1909/1910), pp.369-370.

30. *Vorwärts*, 30 August 1910, 3d supplement, p.1; *Die Gleichheit*, 20 1909/1910), p.389; 21 (1910/1911), p.9.

31. Clara Zetkin to the women comrades, [n.d.], Nachlass Clara Zetkin NY 4005/107 SAPMO-BArch (sheet 3); Aufruf zum Internationalen Sozialistenkongreß zu Basel (November 1912), reprinted in Clara Zetkin, *Ausgewählte Reden und Schriften* (Berlin, 1957), pp.561-563.

32. *Congrès extraordinaire 1912*, pp.134-136 (emphasis in the original).

33. Zetkin to Heleen Ankersmit, 3 December 1914, Nachlass Clara Zetkin NY 4005/69 SAPMO-BArch (sheets 36, 38, 43).

34. Zetkin to Ankersmit, 3 December 1914, Nachlass Clara Zetkin NY 4005/69 SAPMO-BArch (sheets 37-38); Agnes Blänsdorf, *Die Zweite Internationale und der Krieg: Die diskussion über die internationale Zusammenarbeit der sozialistischen Parteien 1914-1917* (Stuttgart, 1979), pp.188f.

35. Eckhard Müller, 'Clara Zetkin und die Internationale Frauenkonferenz im März 1915 in Bern', in *Clara Zetkin in ihrer Zeit. Neue Fakten, Erkenntnisse, Wertungen. Material des Kolloquiums anlässlich ihres 150. Geburtstages am 6. Juli 2007 in Berlin*, ed. Ulla Plener (Rosa-Luxemburg-Stiftung Manuskripte 76) (Berlin, 2008), pp.54-71, 57-59 (including original quote).

36. Bolshevik representatives voted against this resolution. II. Internationale RY 4/ I 6/2/69, SAPMO-BArch (sheets 3-4); *Arbeiter-innenzeitung*, 24 (1915) 3; 4; 5, pp.2-3.; 7, pp.2-3; Gilbert Badia, *Clara Zetkin. Eine neue Biographie* (Berlin, 1994), p.141; Müller, 'Clara Zetkin', p.60; Johanna M Welcker, 'Ankersmit, Gerda Johanna Helena', *Biografisch Woordenboek van het Socialisme en de Arbeidersbeweging in Nederland* (1990), http://www.iisg.nl/bwsa/bios/ankersmit-g.html (accessed 10/7/2010).

37. Zetkin to Ankersmit, 16 January 1915, 4 February 1915, 9 February 1915, 13 March 1915, Nachlass Clara Zetkin NY 4005/69, SAPMO-BArch (sheets 50-51, 55-58).

38. Various versions (with different emphases) are preserved in II. Internationale RY 4/ I 6/2/69, SAPMO-BArch (sheet 13); and Nachlass Clara Zetkin NY 4005/69, SAPMO-BArch (sheets 15-16).

39. II. Internationale RY 4/ I 6/2/69, SAPMO-BArch (sheets 5-6).

40. Archival sources and secondary literature contain contradictory information and claims regarding the voting behaviour of the Bolshevist minority. II. Internationale RY 4/ I 6/2/69, SAPMO-BArch (sheets 1-4); Adelheid Popp, *Der Weg zur Höhe. Die sozialdemokratische Frauenbewegung Österreichs* (Vienna, 1929), pp.122-123; Victor Adler, *Briefwechsel mit August Bebel und Karl Kautsky sowie Briefe von und an Ignaz Auer, Eduard Bernstein, Adolf Braun, Heinrich Dietz, Friedrich Ebert, Wilhelm Liebknecht, Hermann Müller und Paul Singer* (Vienna, 1954), pp.617-618; Blänsdorf, *Die Zweite Internationale und der Krieg*, p.203; Craig Nation, *War on War: Lenin, the Zimmerwald left, and the origins of communist internationalism* (London, 1989), pp.68-69; Merle Fainsod, *International Socialism and the World War* (New York, 1966) pp.56-57; Müller, 'Clara Zetkin', pp.64-66; Welcker, 'Ankersmit'.

41. I am grateful to Natalia Gafizova for the latter information based on her knowledge of Russian sources. II. Internationale RY 4/ I 6/2/69

APMO-BArch (sheets 1-5), contains conference minutes as endorsed y the majority (and including the Bolshevik draft resolution).

.fterword

. For an account of my Zetkin-related research experiences in Germa-y, eastern and western, see Partington, 'On the Trail of Clara Zetkin', 'ounterfire, 16 April 2010, http://www.counterfire.org/ idex.php/features/75-our-history/4654-on-the-trail-of-clara-zetkin iccessed 28 July 2011).

. Zetkin's selected writings appeared as *Clara Zetkin: Ausgewählte 'eden und Schriften*, 3 vols (Berlin, 1957-1960), edited by the Institut ir Marxismus-Leninismus beim ZK der SED. For other writings by etkin published in the GDR, and for biographies and critical works, ee the chapter by Florence Hervé in the present volume.

. At a popular level, an FRG exception existed (and exists) in the tuttgart suburb of Sillenbuch, where the Waldheim Stuttgart e.V. ;lara-Zetkin-Haus' operates. Zetkin had a home in Sillenbuch from 903 to 1929 (though after 1920 she spent most of her time in the oviet Union) and she helped found the Waldheim Stuttgart (a kind of olitical and recreational commune) in 1909. The Waldheim was re-amed in her honour in 1972, and has continued to celebrate her life nd ideas. See Adele Sperandio, Elke Günther and Claudio Sperandio, 'lara Zetkin und Rosa Luxemburg in Stuttgart-Sillenbuch. Die Zeit um 907 (Stuttgart: Claudio Sperandio, 1996). For an account of the /aldheim's continued interest in Zetkin, see Partington, 'On the Trail f Clara Zetkin'.

The Socialist History Society

he Socialist History Society was founded in 1992 and includes many ading Socialist and labour historians, academic and amateur searchers, in Britain and overseas. The SHS holds regular events, ublic meetings and seminars, and contributes to current historical ebates and controversies. We produce a range of publications, including 1e journal *Socialist History* and a regular Newsletter.

The SHS is the successor to the Communist Party History Group, hich was established in 1946 and is now totally independent of all olitical parties and groups. We are engaged in and seek to encourage istorical studies from a Marxist and broadly-defined left perspective. We re interested in all aspects of human history from the earliest social ormations to the present day and aim for an international approach.

We are particularly interested in the various struggles of labour, of omen, of progressive campaigns and peace movements around the orld, as well as the history of colonial peoples, black people, and all ppressed communities seeking justice, human dignity and liberation.

Each year we produce two issues of our journal *Socialist History,* one r two historical pamphlets in our *Occasional Publications* series, and equent members' Newsletters. We hold public lectures and seminars ainly in London. In addition, we hold special conferences, book unches and joint events with other friendly groups.

oin the Socialist History Society today!

lembers receive all our serial publications for the year at no extra cost nd regular mailings about our activities. Members can vote at our AGM nd seek election to positions on the committee, and are encouraged to articipate in other society activities.

nnual membership fees for 2013 (renewable every January):

ull UK	£25.00
oncessionary UK	£18.00
urope full	£30.00
urope concessionary	£24.00
est of world full	£35.00
est of world concessionary	£29.00

For details of institutional subscriptions, please e-mail the Treasurer n francis@socialisthistorysociety.co.uk.

To join the society for 2013, please send your name and address plus cheque/PO payable to **Socialist History Society** to: SHS, 50 Elmfield load, Balham, London SW17 8AL. You can also pay online. 'isit our websites on www.socialisthistorysociety.co.uk and ww.socialist-history-journal.org.uk.